ESSENCE OF SPIRITUAL WISDOM

Inspirational Thoughts of Western Masters

This collection of quotations can serve as medicine if they are imbibed repeatedly. They can help one feel good about oneself and life in general. A good quote can be worth thousand words if conveyed logically and according to the context.

GEMS OF WISDOM

R.K. Jain (Ed.)

ESSENCE OF SPIRITUAL WISDOM

Inspirational Thoughts of Eastern Masters

Compiled by

Rupali Segal • Anirudh Vasdev

ESSENCE OF SPIRITUAL WISDOM

Inspirational Thoughts of Western Masters

Compiled by

Neha Khandelwal

ESSENCE OF SPIRITUAL WISDOM

Inspirational Thoughts of Western Masters

Compiled by

NEHA KHANDELWAL

New Age Books

New Delhi (India)

GEMS OF WISDOM

ESSENCE OF SPIRITUAL WISDOM

Inspirational Thoughts of Western Masters

ISBN: 978-81-7822-450-3 (Series)
ISBN: 978-81-7822-478-7

First Edition: Delhi, **2018**

Published by
NEW AGE BOOKS
A-44 Naraina Industrial Area, Phase-I
New Delhi (India)- 110028)
E-mail: nab@newagebooksindia.com
Website: www.newagebooksindia.com

NAB Cataloging-in-Publication Data
Khandelwal, Neha
ISBN 978-81-7822-478-7
Includes Introduction, Conclusion
Spirituality

Published by
RP Jain for New Age Books
A-44, Naraina Industrial Area Phase-I,
New Delhi-110028. India
Printed by Replika Press Pvt. Ltd.

PREFACE

Sometimes one just needs a bit of inspiration or motivation to get the day going. Such inspiration can come from anywhere, colleagues, parents, friends or even strangers! That is why those who can inspire or motivate people are always looked in good esteem in every walk of life. These people when they share their wisdom with common folk are celebrated as spiritual masters. The company of such spiritual masters enliven people as they find their sermons, preaching or even general talk spiritually uplifting.

However, due to paucity of times and busy life it is not possible for everybody to be in the physical presence of such masters. Therefore here in this book I have culled some of the best inspirational quotes which are full of wit, humour and motivation from various sources. The quotations have been arranged here thematically representing a broad spectrum of spiritual traditions of West. They range from Jesus to John Milton, Archemidies to Einstein, Wordsworth to Al–Ghazali, Alexander to Napoleon. The wise words of these masters of their field have trickled down through ages propagating truth and knowledge which are not something one can find in school textbooks or college classrooms. They are within us. The challenge is to realize them.

These quotes can serve as medicine if imbibed repeatedly. They can help one feel good about oneself and life in general. A good quote can be worth thousand words if conveyed logically and according to the context.

Quotations help to remember a point or lesson because through the power of imagination and visualization the brain responds immediately. These quotes are very memorable and can be carried all the times. Verily this inspirational book is meant for every generation, both young and old.

Finally, I'd like to thank few chosen ones who have been inspirational for me to take up this literary journey. First and foremost, I should express my deep sense of gratitude to the Publisher, who saw the spiritual spark within me. This book would not have come to the light without his support and encouragement. I am also grateful to Jyotsna Khandelwal for investing her trust on me to do such a great work to inspire others.

Neha Khandelwal

PUBLISHER'S NOTE

We believe that in today's fast and hectic life, we seldom find time to reflect on life's myriad mysteries. But we must set aside some time to consciously cultivate contemplation to understand the purpose of life and, more importantly, ourselves. For this, we may seek wisdom from the lives and teachings of the great masters who have inspired millions with their words of wisdom. We therefore thought that their sayings or quotations should be compiled which would inspire and also enlighten us. After the great success of *Essence of Spiritual Wisdom: Inspirational Thoughts from Eastern Masters* we have compiled in this book the quotations of the Western Masters which capture the essence of spiritual wisdom. They would help us to discover ourselves.

We would like to dedicate this book to all those who have helped us, directly or indirectly. While it's impossible to include the names of everyone, a few people deserve special mention. Neha, who has always been fond of writing spiritual quotes since her school days, has compiled the quotations. We're thankful for her labour of love. We're also thankful to Mr R K Jain for his valuable advice and guidance; and to Jyotsna for her helpful comments, enthusiasm and for producing this book elegantly.

CONTENTS

Preface v
Publisher's Note vii
Abundance 1
Acceptance 1
Action 2
Adversity 4
Advice 5
Ambition 7
Anger 8
Anxiety 11
Apathy/Inertia 12
Atheism 12
Awakening/Awareness 13
Beauty 14
Belief 15
Body 16
Cause & Effect 17
Change 19
Character 21
Charity 23
Children 23
Choice 26
Conscience 27
Consciousness 28
Contentment 28
Courage 29
Death 30
Depression/Despair 35
Desire 37
Devil 39
Discipline 40
Doubt 42
Dreams 44
Duality 46
Ego/Vanity 47
Emotions 50
Enemy 52
Energy 54
Enlightenment 55
Enthusiasm 55
Envy/Jealousy 57
Evil 58
Example 60
Failure/Mistake 61
Faith 64
Falsehood 66
Fame 67
Fate/Destiny 68
Fault-Finding 69
Fear 71
Forgiveness 73
Freedom 74
Friendship 76
Genius 77
Giving 78
Goals 81
God 81
God's Will 84
Golden Rule 86
Good 86
Grace 88
Gratitude 89
Greatness 90
Grief 91
Growth 92
Habits 93
Happiness 95
Hatred 98
Health 99
Heart 100
Heaven & Hell 101
Here & Now 103

Humility 104
Hypocrisy 106
Ignorance 107
Illusions 109
Imagination 110
Imitation 111
Immortality/Eternity 112
Journey 112
Joy 114
Judgement 115
Kindness/Gentleness 116
Laughter 117
Lesson 118
Life 119
Light 122
Little 124
Loneliness 125
Love 126
Meditation 130
Mind 131
Miracles 133
Moderation 134
Money 134
Nature 136
Nothing/Emptiness 137
Old Age 138
Oneness 140
Order 142
Pain 142
Past 144
Patience 145
Peace/Harmony 146
Perfection 148
Perseverance 150
Pessimism 151
Possessions 152
Power 153
Prayer 155
Pride 157
Principle 158
Problems 159
Prosperity 160
Purpose 161
Relationship 161
Religion 164
Saints 165
Search/Look Within 166
Self-Esteem 168
Selfishness 169
Self-Realization 170
Self-Reliance 170
Service 171
Silence 173
Simplicity 174
Smile 175
Solitude 177
Speech 179
Spirituality 180
Success 181
Suffering 183
Surrender 185
Teacher 185
Thoughts 186
Time 188
Truth 189
War 191
Wealth 193
Wisdom 194
Words 195
Work 197
Worry 198

Abundance

If there is but little water in the stream, it is the fault, not of the channel, but of the source... —*St. Jerome*

To him that has, more shall be given; but from him that has not, the little that he has shall be taken away... —*Jesus*

There is enough of everything for everyone... —*Patricia Sun*

Abundance consists not so much in material possessions, but in an uncovetous spirit... —*John Selden*

Abundance is scooped from abundance yet abundance remains... —*Anne Sexton*

Too often we visit the well of divine abundance with a teacup instead of a bucket... —*Elinor MacDonald*

God is able to provide you with every blessing in abundance... —*Paul of Tarsus*

Acceptance

When God sends rain...rain is my choice... —*James W. Riley*

Acceptance is a letting–go process. You let go of your wishes and demands that life can be different. It's a conscious choice... —*Gary Emery*

Acceptance of one's life has nothing to do with resignation; it does not mean running away from the struggle. On the contrary it means accepting it as it comes...To accept is to say yes to life in its entirety... —*Paul Tournier*

Rowing against the tide is hard and uncertain. To go with

the tide and thus take advantage of the workings of the great natural force is safe and easy... —*Ralph W. Trine*

Action

Action springs out of what we fundamentally desire...
—*Harry A. Overstreet*

Creativity is "doing," and it burns itself out; its end is exhaustion...
—*William Gibson*

Inaction may be the highest form of action... —*Jerry Brown*

Steady, determined and purposeful action is one prayer always answered...
—*Norman Thornton*

Trust only movement. Life happens at the level of events, not of words...
—*Alfred Adler*

Knowing is not enough; we must apply! Waiting is not enough; we must do...
—*Johann W. Goethe*

Between saying and doing many shoes are worn out...
—*Italian saying*

We get to know the things we are attempting to master only by doing them. No amount of teaching or study ever made a craftsman...
—*U.S. Anderson*

When a man acts wisely, he grows old slowly. When he acts unwisely, he grows older and older every day in every way...
—*Fred Van Amburgh*

Do what you can, with what you have, where you are...
—*Theodore Roosevelt*

Leadership is action, not position... —*Donald H. McGannon*

Our deeds determine us, as much as we determine our deeds...
—*George Eliot*

Action is the single most effective antidote to depression,

anxiety, stress, fear, wrong, guilt and of course, immobility. It is virtually impossible to be depressed and active at the same time... —*Wayne Dyer*

He who moves not forward goes backward...
—*Johann W. Goethe*

Experience is the child of thought, and thought is the child of action. We cannot learn from books...
—*Benjamin Disraeli*

Concern should drive us into action and not into depression... —*Karen Horney*

Wisdom without action hath its seat in the mouth; but by means of action, it becomes fixed in the heart...
—*Shekel Hakodesh*

Every action of our lives touches on some chord that will vibrate into eternity... —*Edwin H. Chapin*

He who desires but acts not, breeds pestilence...
—*William Blake*

Every man without passions has within him no principle of action, nor motive to act... —*Claude A. Helvetius*

I find the great thing in this world is not so much where we stand, as in what direction we are moving...—*Oliver W. Holmes*

A little knowledge which you carry into action is more profitable than much knowledge which you neglect to carry out into action... —*Hermes*

Heaven never helps the man who will not act... —*Sophocles*

The basis of action is the lack of imagination. It is the last resource of those who know not how to dream...—*Oscar Wilde*

An ounce of action is worth a ton of theory... —*Friedrich Engels*

Great thoughts reduced to practice become great acts...
—*William Hazlitt*

The actions of men are the best interpreters of their thoughts... —*John Locke*

We are not to lead events but follow them... —*Epictetus*

The busy bee has no time for sorrow... —*William Blake*

Adversity

Bad times have a scientific value. These are occasions a good learner would not miss... —*Ralph W. Emerson*

The bravest sight in the world is to see a great man struggling against adversity... —*Seneca*

You get tragedy where the tree, instead of bending, breaks...
—*Ludwig Wittgenstein*

Difficulty...is the nurse of greatness---a harsh nurse, who roughly rocks her foster children into strength and athletic proportion... —*William C. Bryant*

Tragedy is like a strong acid–it dissolves away all but the very gold of truth... —*D.H. Lawrence*

The positive and victorious attitude keeps adversity away, while a negative attitude attracts it... —*Henry T. Hamblin*

One of the secrets of life is making stepping stones out of stumbling blocks... —*Jack Penn*

Meet adversity by turning defeat into victory...
—*John A. Schindler*

Adversity is the first path of truth... —*George Byron*

Adversity? It's a tonic, not a stumbling block! Every adversity carries the seed of an equal or greater benefit...
—*Napoleon Hill*

Many things are learned in adversity which the prosperous man never dreams of... —*Charles H. Spurgeon*

Adversity has the effect of eliciting talents which in prosperous times would have lain dormant... —*Horace*

Fire is the test of gold; adversity of strong men... —*Seneca*

Adversity is the trial of principle. Without it a man hardly knows whether he is honest or not... —*Henry Fielding*

We're like tea bags: We don't know our strength until we get into hot water... —*Bruce Laingen*

An undisturbed mind is the best sauce for adversity... —*Plautus*

Adversity is the midwife of genius... —*Napoleon Bonaparte*

Adversity is a severe instructor, set over us by one who knows better than we do ourselves... —*Edmund Burke*

The winds and the waves are always on the side of the ablest navigators... —*Edward Gibbon*

He who has no cross will have no crown... —*Francis Quarles*

For trouble is the thing that strong men grow by... —*H. Bertram Lewis*

If you lose heart when adversity comes, your strength will only be weakness... —*Old Testament*

Sometimes great difficulties are permitted only in order to strengthen the character... —*Robert Benson*

Advice

The true secret of giving advice is, after you have honestly given it, to be perfectly indifferent whether it is taken or not... —*Hannah W. Smith*

All the advice in the world will never help you until you help yourself... —*Fred Van Amburgh*

Nobody gives you wiser advice than yourself... —*Cicero*

Advice is like castor oil, easy enough to give but dreadful uneasy to take... —*Henry W. Shaw*

Whoever gives advice to a heedless man is himself in need of advice... —*Saadi*

Advice is worth what it costs–that is, nothing... —*Douglas MacArthur*

When a man seeks your advice he generally wants your praise... —*Philip Chesterfield*

Men give away nothing so liberally as their advice... —*Francois La Rochefoucauld*

Giving advice is sometimes only showing our wisdom at the expense of another... —*Anthony Shaftesbury*

Whatever advice you give, be brief... —*Horace*

A good scare is worth more to a man than good advice... —*Edgar W. Howe*

Advice is what we ask for when we already know the answer but wish we didn't... —*Erica Jong*

How is it possible to expect mankind to take advice when they will not so much as take warning?... —*Jonathan Swift*

Many receive advice, few profit from it.... —*Publilius Syrus*

He who can take advice is sometimes superior to him who can give it... —*Karl von Knebel*

Advice is seldom welcome; those who need it most, like it least... —*Samuel Johnson*

Before giving advice we must have secured its acceptance,

or rather, have made it desired... —*Henry F. Amiel*

Ambition

To be unhappy at home is the ultimate result of all ambition... —*Ben Johnson*

The ambitious climb up high and perilous stairs, and never care how to come down... —*Thomas Adams*

A slave has one master; an ambitious man has many masters... —*Jean La Bruyere*

Ambition is not a vice of little people... —*Michel Montaigne*

Ambition is but the evil shadow of aspiration...
—*George MacDonald*

Ambition is the grand enemy of all peace, inner as well as outer... —*John Cowper Powys*

Ambition is bubbles on the rapid stream of life...
—*Edward Young*

Ambition breaks the ties of blood and forges the obligations of gratitude... —*Walter Scott*

Ambition is the avarice of power; and happiness herself is soon sacrificed to that very lust of dominion...
—*Charles C. Colton*

Most of the trouble in the world is caused by people wanting to be important... —*T.S. Eliot*

Ambition is like love, impatient of delays and rivals...
—*John Denham*

Ambition and suspicion always go together...
—*Georg C. Lichtenberg*

Ambition is a condition inspired by the wish to be first...
—*Max Gralnick*

Ambition is so powerful a passion in the human breast, that however high we reach we are never satisfied...
—Niccolo Machiavelli

Ambition is bondage... *—Solomon Ibn Gabirol*

Life gets more tranquil when the ambitions die away...
—Lord Birket

If we do not encourage our ambition, feed it and strengthen it by vigorous exercise, it will soon die...
—Orison A. Marden

Ambition is the senseless chasing of rainbows...
—Frederick Loewe

Discontent follows ambition like a shadow...
—Henry S. Hawkins

Most people would succeed in small things, if they were not troubled with great ambitions... *—Henry W. Longfellow*

Throw away all ambition beyond that of doing the day's work well... *—William Osler*

Ambition destroys its possessor... *—The Talmud*

Ambition becomes displeasing once it is satisfied...
—Pierre Corneille

Anger

It is not what we say that hurts but how we say it...
—John Gray

Anger and hatred are the materials from which hell is made...
—Thich Nhat Hanh

Always shun whatever makes you angry... *—Publilius Syrus*

Anger is the emotion preeminently serviceable for the display of power... *—Walter B. Cannon*

We must interpret a bad temper as the sign of an inferiority complex... —*Alfred Adler*

Anger insures that one gives oneself up to one's enemies blindly... —*Eliphas Levi*

Anger helps straighten out a problem like a fan helps straighten out a pile of papers... —*Susan Marcotte*

Expressing anger when you feel angry nearly always makes you angrier... —*Carol Tavris*

Hesitation is the best cure for anger. The first blows of anger are heavy, but if it waits, it will think again... —*Seneca*

When a sage is angry, he is no longer a sage...
—*The Talmud*

Strong negative emotions like anger, irritation, and indignation usually, but not always, indicate that our weak spot has been touched consciously or unconsciously...
—*Fritz Kunkel*

An unawakened person uses "anger" as a screen to hide fear, insecurity and a guilty conscience... —*Ot Lat Nom*

When angry, count to ten before you speak; if very angry, one hundred... —*Thomas Jefferson*

Anger is momentary madness... —*Horace*

Whenever you are angry, be assured that it is not only a present evil, but you have increased a habit, added fuel to a fire... —*Epictetus*

To be angry is to revenge the faults of others upon ourselves... —*Alexander Pope*

The angry man always thinks he can do more than he can...
—*Albertano of Brescia*

Anger is...an alarm system, signaling the presence of nothing more than fear. It tells us we are working at cross-purposes to our own happiness, fearing the loss of something more than we enjoy the experience of having it...

—Jesse Jennings

For every minute you are angry you lose sixty seconds of happiness... *—Ralph W. Emerson*

Anger may aptly be compared to cancer. It is, in fact, mental carcinoma. In its effects it is more deadly to the mind than cancer is to the body... *—Julian P. Johnson*

Anger is the wind which blows out the lamp of the mind...

—Robert Ingersoll

Anger is a form of fear and evidence of the need of defence... *—Fred Van Amburgh*

Anger is the most impotent of passions. It effects nothing as it goes about, and hurts the one who is possessed by it more than the one against whom it is directed...

—Edward Clarendon

Whenever you hold resentment toward another, you are bound to that person or condition by an emotional link that is stronger than steel... *—Catherine Ponder*

An angry man opens his mouth and closes his eyes...

—Cato the Elder

He best keeps from anger who remembers that God is always looking at him... *—Plato*

Many people lose their tempers merely from seeing you keep yours... *—Frank M. Colby*

He whose face is inflamed with anger shows the evil spirit burns within him... *—The Zohar*

When a man is wrong and won't admit it, he gets angry...

—Thomas Haliburton

Anger leads to hatred, to scapegoats, to violence, to destruction... —*Jesse Jackson*

When one obeys anger in his life he will reap only pain and anguish. No one can follow the habit of anger and make any progress on the spiritual path... —*Paul Twitchell*

Anger repressed can poison a relationship as surely as the cruelest words... —*Joyce Brothers*

The intoxication of anger, like that of the grape, shows us to others, but hides us from ourselves... —*Charles C. Colton*

To rule one's anger is well; to prevent it is still better... —*Tryon Edwards*

Anxiety

Anxiety is the price of freedom... —*Sören Kierkegaard*

Anxiety is the dread of nothingness... —*Martin Heidegger*

Anxiety is the mark of spiritual insecurity... —*Thomas Merton*

Anxiety is the poison of human life; the parent of many sins and more miseries... —*Hugh Blair*

Anxiety in the heart...causes depression, but a good word makes it glad... —*Old Testament*

God did not make us to be eaten by anxiety, but to walk erect, free, unafraid in a world where there is work to do, truth to seek, love to give and win... —*Joseph Newton*

Anxiety is fear of one's self... —*Wilhelm Stekel*

Beware of anxiety...there is nothing that so much troubles the mind, strains the heart, distresses the soul and confuses the judgement... —*William B. Ullathorne*

Do you wish to live in tension? By no means. No one who is

in a state of fear or sorrow or tension is free, but whoever is delivered from sorrows or fears or anxieties, he is at the same time delivered from servitude... —*Epictetus*

Apathy/Inertia

I would rather attempt to do something great and fail, than attempt to do nothing and succeed... —*Robert Schuller*

The man who makes no mistakes does not usually make anything... —*W.C. Magee*

The force that opposes determination is inertia. Inertia is not a static thing; it is a dynamic force. Like any force, it tends to magnify itself and gain momentum until or unless it is superseded by another force stronger than itself...
—*Alan Cohen*

The great thing in this world is not so much where we stand, as in what direction we are moving... —*Oliver W. Holmes*

There is something worse than a difficulty. It is inertia. If you try to escape difficulties, you decay... —*Herbert Casson*

The greatest mistake a man can make is to be afraid of making one... —*Elbert Hubbard*

Atheism

An atheist is a man who believes himself an accident...
—*Francis Thompson*

The absolute affirmation of evil is the denial of God, since God is the supreme and absolute source of life...
—*Eliphas Levi*

There is really no such thing as an atheist. Atheists think they exist, but in God's reality they do not exist...
—*Peace Pilgrim*

No one has ever died an atheist...Few men are so obstinate

in their atheism, that a pressing danger will not compel them to the knowledge of a divine power... —*Plato*

An atheist is a man who has no invisible means of support... —*John Buchan*

The worst moment for an atheist is when he feels grateful and doesn't know who to thank... —*Wendy Ward*

No man hates God without first hating himself... —*Fulton J. Sheen*

Awakening/Awareness

Awareness and happiness are exactly the same thing... —*Vernon Howard*

Most are asleep as to their spiritual destiny, but they will one day awaken to it... —*Darwin Gross*

To those who are awake, there is one ordered universe, whereas in sleep each person turns away from the world to one of his own... —*Heraclitus*

The aim of life is to live, and to live means to be aware, joyously, drunkenly, serenely, divinely aware... —*Henry Miller*

The man who is aware of himself is henceforth independent... —*Virginia Woolf*

An aware person is in tune with all the powers of God and makes them his own... —*Donald Curtis*

The most powerful agent in character building is the awakening of the true self to the fact that man is a spiritual being... —*Ralph W. Trine*

Only when you awaken do you realize you were dreaming... —*John Wareham*

If I were to begin life again, I should want it as it was. I would only open my eyes a little more... *—Jules Renard*

Awareness means the capacity to see a coffeepot and hear the birds sing in one's own way and not the way one was taught... *—Eric Berne*

The real voyage of discovery consists not in seeking new landscapes but in having new eyes... *—Marcel Proust*

It's the awareness...of how you are stuck, that makes you recover... *—Fritz Perls*

Beauty

Beauty is one of those rare things that does not lead to the doubt of God... *—Jean Anouilh*

There is no physical barrier to experiencing yourself as beautiful, only your belief... *—Harold H. Bloomfield*

Beauty you may have with you always, if you will but plant beauty in your heart... *—Fred Van Amburgh*

We are living in a world of beauty, but few of us open our eyes to see it... *—Lorado Taft*

Beauty fades, but a good name endures...
—Apocrypha: Ahikar

Beauty is merely the spiritual making itself known sensuously... *—Georg W. Hegel*

Never lose an opportunity of seeing anything that is beautiful; for beauty is God's handwriting—a wayside sacrament. Welcome it in every fair face, in every fair sky, in every fair flower, and thank God for it as a cup of blessing...
—Ralph W. Emerson

Things are beautiful if you love them... *—Jean Anouilh*

What is beautiful is good, and who is good will soon also be beautiful... *—Sappho*

Everything that is true is beautiful... —*Eliphas Levi*

Belief

Believe in poverty and you will be poor. Believe in wealth and you will be rich. Believe in love and you will have love. Believe in health and you will be healthy... —*Napoleon Hill*

To believe is to be strong. Doubt cramps energy. Belief is power... —*Frederick W. Robertson*

A belief is like a guillotine, just as heavy, just as light... —*Franz Kafka*

We can be victimized by our beliefs... —*Judy Tatelbaum*

As our beliefs actually change, so do our experiences... —*Carol Sheffield*

To believe in the things you see and touch is no belief at all; but to believe in the unseen is a triumph and a blessing... —*Abraham Lincoln*

The essence of belief is the establishment of habit... —*Charles S. Pearce*

One person with a belief is equal to a force of ninety nine who only have interests... —*John S. Mill*

One does not have to believe everything one hears... —*Cicero*

A belief is not merely an idea the mind possesses; it is an idea that possesses the mind... —*Robert Bolton*

Whatsoever things you desire, believe and you shall have them... —*Jesus*

Where belief is painful, we are slow to believe... —*Ovid*

Body

Death is a shadow that always follow the body...
—*English proverb*

The soul is a guest in our body, deserving of our kind hospitality... —*Hillel*

The body has one fault, that the more people pamper it, the more its wants are made known... —*Teresa of Avila*

The body exists, by nature, in a condition of well-being. It is a place to observe the world from. It is a physical representation of you, and it is not you... —*Ron Smothermon*

The human body has one ability not possessed by any machine—the ability to repair itself... —*George W. Crile*

Our minds have unbelievable power over our bodies...
—*André Maurois*

All of us have mortal bodies, composed of perishable matter, but the soul lives forever: it is a portion of the Deity housed in our bodies... —*Flavius Josephus*

The body without the spirit is death... —*Paul of Tarsus*

So great a power is there of the soul upon the body, that whichever way the soul imagines and dreams that it goes, thither doth it lead the body... —*Marcus Agrippa*

The body is a workhouse of the soul... —*Henry G. Bohn*

A healthy body is a guest chamber for the soul; a sick body is a prison... —*Francis Bacon*

My body is merely a clay structure; today it is here, tomorrow it shall be gone... —*Peace Pilgrim*

The body is the soul's house. Shouldn't we take care of our house that it doesn't fall into ruin?... —*Philo*

Cause & Effect

If men spit upon the ground, they spit upon themselves...
—*Chief Seattle*

In this world everything changes except good deeds and bad deeds; these follow you as the shadows follow the body...
—*Ruth Benedict*

A perfect cause must produce a perfect effect...
—*Ernest Holmes*

In all human affairs there are efforts, and there are results, and the strength of the effort is the measure of the result. Chance is not...
—*James Allen*

The cause is hidden, but the result is known...
—*Ovid*

A great flame follows a little spark...
—*Dante Alighieri*

If you help others, you will be helped, perhaps tomorrow, perhaps in one hundred years, but you will be helped. Nature must pay off the debt...it is a mathematical law and all life is mathematics...
—*George I. Gurdjieff*

Cause and effect, means and ends, seed and fruit, cannot be severed; for the effect already blooms in the cause, the end pre-exists in the means, the fruit in the seed...You cannot do wrong without suffering wrong...
—*Ralph W. Emerson*

One who knows the cause knows the effect. But the cause of human effects is the heart...
—*Thomas Aquinas*

No man in the world ever attempted to wrong another without being injured in return—some way, somehow, sometime. Nature keeps her books admirably; she puts down every item, she closes all accounts finally, but she does not always balance them at the end of the month...
—*William G. Jordan*

We sow our thoughts, and we reap our actions; we sow our actions, and we reap our habits; we sow our habits, we reap our characters; we sow our characters and reap our destiny...

—C.A. Hall

The present condition continues nothing more than the past, and what is found in the effect was already in the cause... *—Henri Bergson*

For every action, there is an equal and opposite reaction. If you push hard on the world, the world pushes back on you. If you touch the world gently, the world will touch you gently in return... *—Paul Hewitt*

Wise is the man who seeks the cause of things...If the market goes up, or if the market goes down, there is a cause. If business is good, or not so, there is a cause. If you are ill, there is a cause... *—Fred Van Amburgh*

Wisdom is the faculty of knowing what will be the effect of a cause... *—Alfred A. Montapert*

Good thoughts and actions never produce bad results; bad thoughts and actions can never produce good results. This is but saying that nothing can come from corn but corn, nothing from nettles but nettles ... *—James Allen*

The world is a looking glass, and gives back to every man the reflection of his own face. Frown at it, and it will in turn look sourly upon you; laugh at it and with it, and it is a jolly, kind companion... *—William M. Thackeray*

All life is a boomerang. We receive what we give...

—Shirley MacLaine

Every seed bears its fruit; the fruit of good deeds is sweet, that of others is always bitter; always remember that...

—Allan Kardec

Through the law of cause and effect we choose our destiny.

Moreover, we are our own prophets, for we constantly project our future state by the seeds we plant in the present...
—*Cheryl Canfield*

No effect is ever the effect of a single cause, but only a combination of causes... —*Herbert Samuel*

Change

Consider how hard it is to change yourself, and what little chance you have of trying to change others...
—*Jacob M. Braude*

The world never stands still. It is a constant becoming. The face of the earth–as well as the face you see in the mirror–offers clear evidence that all is flux and change...
—*Robert Collier*

Not everything that is faced can be changed, but nothing can be changed until it is faced... —*James Baldwin*

All things change, creeds and philosophies and outward systems–but God remains!... —*Mrs. Humphry Ward*

The absurd man is he who never changes...
—*Auguste Barthelemy*

All our resolves and decisions are made in a mood or frame of mind which is certain to change... —*Marcel Proust*

Some people change when they see the light; others when they feel the heat... —*Caroline Schroeder*

If you want to truly understand something, try to change it... —*Kurt Lewin*

There is nothing that stands fast, nothing fixed, nothing free from change, among the things which come into being, neither among those in heaven nor among those on earth. God alone stands unmoved... —*Hermes*

If you don't like something about yourself, change it. If you can't change it, then accept it... —*Ted Shackelford*

There are no quick fixes that can permanently change your life... —*Sonya Friedman*

It is useless and futile to try to change other people. The only person I can change is myself... —*William Curtiss*

Change, indeed is painful, yet ever needful...
—*Thomas Carlyle*

All things must change to something new, to something strange... —*Henry W. Longfellow*

Change is always more complicated than most of us imagine...Even when you are highly motivated to change, it is difficult to do so. Years have gone into building who we are, and worse than anything it is scary to rearrange our parts... —*Melvyn Kinder*

Change is one thing, progress is another... —*Lord Russell*

There is a strict rule in spiritual life that every change, each experience, comes only when the person is ripe...
—*Lucy Cornellssen*

The main dangers in this life are the people who want to change everything...or nothing... —*Lady Astor*

Change is our ally... —*Willard Wirtz*

Progress is impossible without change; and those who cannot change their minds cannot change anything...
—*George B. Shaw*

The wood does not change the fire into itself, but the fire changes the wood into itself. So we are changed into God, that we shall know Him as He is... —*Meister Eckhart*

The world hates change; yet it is the only thing that has

brought progress... —*Charles F. Kettering*

The more things change, the more they remain the same... —*Alphonse Karr*

Change is not made without inconvenience, even from worst to best... —*Richard Hooker*

The man who never alters his opinion is like a man standing in water, and breeds reptiles in his mind... —*William Blake*

We can change, slowly and steadily, if we set our will to it... —*Robert Benson*

Times change and we change with them... —*Raphael Holinshed*

Today is not yesterday. We ourselves change. How then, can our works and thoughts...continue always the same?... —*Thomas Carlyle*

All is flux, nothing stands still. Nothing endures but change...You could not step twice into the same river, for other waters are ever flowing onto you. There is nothing permanent except change... —*Heraclitus*

Character

Character is like a tree and reputation like its shadow. The shadow is what we think of it; the tree is the real thing... —*Abraham Lincoln*

Character builds slowly, but it can be torn down with incredible swiftness... —*Faith Baldwin*

No one can climb out beyond the limitations of his own character... —*John Morley*

No change of circumstance can repair a defect of character... —*Ralph W. Emerson*

Character is much easier kept than recovered...
—Thomas Paine

A man's own character is the arbiter of his fortune...
—Publilius Syrus

Character is not made in a crisis–it is only exhibited...
—Robert Freeman

Character is what you are in the dark... *—Dwight L. Moody*

Character is the result of two things—mental attitude and the way we spend our time... *—Elbert Hubbard*

If I keep my good character, I shall be rich enough...
—Platonicus

You can't give character to another person, but you can encourage him to develop his own by possessing one yourself...
—Artemus Calloway

Let us not say, Every man is the architect of his own fortune; but let us say, Every man is the architect of his own character... *—George Boardman*

High aims form high character... *—Tryon Edwards*

When wealth is lost, noting is lost; when health is lost, something is lost; when character is lost, all is lost...
—German proverb

Character is the spiritual house in which we live...
—Faith Baldwin

Character is that which can do without success...
—Ralph W. Emerson

Talent develops in quiet, character in the torrent of the world... *—Johann W. Goethe*

Charity

One should never expect any other reward from charity than the satisfaction it gives... —*Darryl F. Zanuck*

Charity is the power of defending that which we know to be indefensible... —*G.K. Chesterton*

How shall we expect charity toward others, when we are uncharitable to ourselves?... —*Thomas Browne*

Charity begins at home... —*Terence*

Be charitable and indulgent to everyone but yourself... —*Joseph Joubert*

Charity is the pure gold which makes us rich in eternal wealth... —*Jean P. Camus*

When a needy person stands at your door, God himself stands at his side... —*Hebrew proverb*

Charity is love; not all love is charity... —*Thomas Aquinas*

Charity is injurious unless it helps the recipient to become independent of it... —*John D. Rockefeller*

Nothing is more pleasing to God than a open hand and a closed mouth... —*Francis Quarles*

Charity is a virtue of the heart, and not of the hands... —*Joseph Addison*

Charity brings to life again those who are spiritually dead... —*Thomas Aquinas*

Your charity is not genuine if your words, no matter how true, are not charitable... —*Jean P. Camus*

Children

Parents wonder why the streams are bitter, when they themselves have spoiled the fountain... —*John Locke*

If you think you are your body, then you think that your children's bodies are extensions of your body. But they are a gift, just like your body is a gift. We don't own them, nor can we control them... —*Stephen Levine*

One of the most responsible things you can do as an adult is become more of a child... —*Wayne Dyer*

Give a little love to a child and you get a great deal back... —*John Ruskin*

Up to a certain age the child has a perfect trust in its parents to supply it with food, clothing and shelter. When it is obliged to provide for itself the trouble begins...Then it trusts hardly anything. That may be the cause of all our trouble, wakefulness included... —*Prentice Mulford*

The child must know that he is a miracle, a miracle that since the beginning of the world there hasn't been, and until the end of the world there will not be another child like him. He is a unique thing, a unique thing from the beginning until the end of the world... —*Pablo Casals*

The great man is he who does not lose his child's heart... —*Menicus*

In every man there is a child hidden–it wants to come out... —*Friedrich W. Nietzsche*

Children are God's apostles—sent forth day by day, to preach of love, and hope and peace... —*James Russell Lowell*

Man is most nearly himself when he achieves the seriousness of a child at play... —*Heraclitus*

This is a truth that children know: If you want joy go back to your creative enthusiasm. Refuse to make life work of anything you cannot fill with magic... —*David Seabury*

Childhood and genius have the same master - organ in common—inquisitiveness... —*Edwin Bulwer-Lytton*

When we are no children, we are already dead...
—Constantin Brancusi

What is childhood but a series of happy delusions?...
—Sydney Smith

Children who are not loved in their very beginnings do not know how to love themselves... *—Marion Woodman*

Children need love, especially when they do not deserve it... *—Harold S. Hubert*

Grown men may learn from very little children, for the hearts of little children are pure, and therefore, the Great Spirit may show to them many things which older people miss...
—Black Elk

When childhood dies, its corpses are called adults...
—Brian Addiss

If you can't hold children in your arms, please hold them in your heart... *—Mother Clara Hale*

You cannot teach a child to take care of himself unless you will let him try to take care of himself. He will make mistakes and out of these mistakes will come his wisdom...
—Henry W. Beecher

Of all people, children are the most imaginative...
—Thomas B. Macaulay

When I was a child, I spoke as a child, I understood as a child, I thought as a child. When I became a man, I put away childish things... *—Paul of Tarsus*

Children enjoy the present because they have neither a past nor a future... *—Jean La Bruyere*

The greatest gifts you can give your children are the roots of responsibility and the wings of independence...
—Denis Waitley

Children require guidance and sympathy far more than instruction...
—Anne Sullivan

Choice

Always there is a desire to accept some things and reject others. Who is making this choice, and with what wisdom?...
—Gerald May

Our greatest power is the power of choice; our greatest freedom lies in the exercise of our power of choice...
—William Curtis

One does not decide in favor of one thing without deciding against another: Nothing is ever achieved or gained without giving up something...
—U.S. Anderson

Whatever you choose will become your experience when you believe in your choice and have faith in the ability of Life to fulfill your desires...
—Jack Addington

Choose always the way that seems best, however rough it may be; custom will soon render it easy and agreeable...
—Pythagoras

Life is change...Growth is optional. Choose wisely...
—Karen K. Clark

We do not choose the day of our birth nor may we choose the day of our death, yet choice is the sovereign faculty of the mind...
—Thornton Wilder

There is a small choice in rotten apples...
—William Shakespeare

God asks no man whether he will accept life. That is not the choice. You must take it. The only choice is how...
—Henry W. Beecher

Life is an endless creative experience and we are making ourselves every moment by every decision we make...
—Kent Nerburn

When choices are taken away, a perfect path remains...
—Bo Lozoff

Nature gives man corn but he must grind it; God gives man a will, but he must make the right choices...
—Fulton J. Sheen

"Many are called but few are chosen." Who makes the choice?...only the ones who are called... *—Frater Achad*

Conscience

Real human progress depends upon a good conscience...
—Albert Einstein

Conscience is the perfect interpreter of life... *—Karl Barth*

The one thing that doesn't abide by majority rule is a person's conscience... *—Harper Lee*

A man that will enjoy a quite conscience must lead a quiet life... *—Philip Chesterton*

The foundation of true joy is in the conscience... *—Seneca*

Be the master of your will, and the slave of your conscience...
—Yiddish saying

Conscience warns us as a friend before it punishes us as a judge... *—Leszczynski Stanislaw*

Conscience and reputation are two things. Conscience is due to yourself, reputation to your neighbour...
—Augustine

Conscience is God to all mortals... *—Menander*

The paradoxical-and tragic-situation of man is that his conscience is weakest when he needed it the most...
—Eric Fromm

Conscience is nothing else but the echo of God's voice within the soul... —*E.B. Hall*

Conscience is the root of all free courage; if a man would be brave, let him obey his conscience... —*James F. Clark*

Conscience: the soft whisper of God in man... —*Edward Young*

Consciousness

A lake that is absolutely calm gives to you a perfect reflection. The moment it becomes disturbed in the least, the reflection is distorted; and if the agitation is increased, the reflection will be completely lost. Your consciousness is the lake... —*James B. Schafer*

There is no coming into consciousness without pain... —*Carl Jung*

Consciousness is the way emptiness knows itself... —*Stephen H. Wolinsky*

Contentment

Contentment is natural wealth, luxury is artificial poverty... —*Socrates*

I am always content with what happens; for I know that what God chooses is better that what I choose... —*Epictetus*

A contented mind is the greatest blessing a man can enjoy in this world... —*Joseph Addison*

You never know what is enough unless you know what is more than enough... —*William Blake*

When we have not what we like, we must like what we have... —*Bussy-Rabutin*

Let him who has enough ask for nothing more... —*Horace*

Discontent is like ink poured into water, which fills the whole fountain full of blackness... *—Owen Felltham*

Contentment is the Philosopher's Stone, that turns all it touches to gold... *—Benjamin Franklin*

Nothing is so bitter that a calm mind cannot find comfort in it... *—Seneca*

Courage

If you don't place your foot on the rope, you'll never cross the chasm. Life is a risk. Change and chance are constants... *—Liz Smith*

The weak in courage are strong in cunning... *—William Blake*

It takes great courage to break with one's past history and stand alone... *—Marion Woodman*

A man of courage is also full of faith... *—Cicero*

Courage leads starward, fear towards death... *—Seneca*

Courage is not the absence of fear but the ability to carry on with dignity in spite of it... *—Scott Turow*

To be loved, and to love, need courage; the courage to judge certain values as of ultimate concern–and to take the jump and stake everything on these values... *—Erich Fromm*

Courge is fear holding on a minute longer... *—George S. Patton*

Courage is doing what you're afraid to do. There can be no courage unless you're scared... *—Eddie Rickenbacker*

A great deal of talent is lost to the world for the want of a little courage... *—Sydney Smith*

Life shrinks or expands in proportion to one's courge... *—Anais Nin*

The greatest test of courage on earth is to bear defeat without losing heart... —*Robert Ingersoll*

Death

Death is going from one room to another, ultimately to the most beautiful room... —*Mendel of Kotzk*

It is difficult to accept death in this society because it is unfamiliar. In spite of the fact that it happens all the time, we never see it... —*Elizabeth Kubler-Ross*

Death is always the great trial. The void that suddenly opens under our feet. It is useless to flee it. We must learn to face it. And also to get around it... —*Martin Grey*

The tragedy of death...is separation, but even separation may not be permanent... —*Elizabeth Gray Vining*

Life is the entrance; death is the exit...—*Bahya Ibn Pakuda*

Death? Why the fuss about death. Use your imagination, try to visualize a world without death...Death is an essential condition of life, not an evil... —*Charlotte P. Gilman*

The wise man is never surprised by death: he is always ready to depart... —*Jean La Fontaine*

Never say about anything, "I have lost it," but only "I have given it back." Is your child dead? It has been given back. Is your wife dead? She has been returned... —*Epictetus*

Death is a doorway of another reality... —*Barbara Harris*

Death will always be among us. We shall never escape it. Dying is part of the process of living. We must not fear it. We must not hide it. We must not ignore it. We must not deny it. Death is... —*Robert W. Buckingham*

Death is nothing more than changing gears in the journey of life... —*Hubert van Zeller*

If you want to die happily, learn to live; if you would live happily, learn to die... *—Celio Calgagnini*

Do not seek death. Death will find you. But seek the road which makes death a fulfillment... *—Dag Hammarskjöld*

Come death, if you will: you cannot divide us; you can only unite us... *—Franz Grillparzer*

After you die, you wear what you are... *—Teresa of Avila*

When you die you lose your body. That is all there is to it. Nothing else is lost... *—P.M.H. Atwater*

The attitude toward death is changing... No longer is it something to be feared, but rather a giving of ourselves to God... *—Clifford Howell*

Death is not the end. It is the beginning. No one you are close to ever dies. There is life everlasting; there is no such thing as death...Death is not a termination but a transition... *—George Anderson*

Dying is easy work compared with living. Dying is a moment's transition; living, a transaction of years... *—Maltbie D. Babcock*

We are all equal in the presence of death...*—Publilius Syrus*

Each man must die alone... *—Blaise Pascal*

Death knocks impartially at the door of the poor man's shop and the prince's palace... *—Horace*

Death in itself is nothing; but we fear to be we know not what, we know not where... *—John Dryden*

Death cannot kill what never dies... *—Thomas Traherne*

The fear of death is the most unjustified of all fears, for there's no risk of accident for someone who's dead... *—Albert Einstein*

Every man knows he will die, but no man wants to believe it... —*Yiddish saying*

The only thing we can take with us from this life is the good that we have done to others... —*Betty J. Eadie*

Death...is but a passing through a dark entry, out of one little dusky room in our Father's house into another that is far and large lightsome and glorious, and divinely entertaining... —*McDonald Clarke*

Death no longer seems the final end it used to be, but rather the entrance to a new and free existence which includes all space and time... —*Charles Lindbergh*

Death is no enemy of man; it is a friend who, when the work of life is done, just cuts the cord that binds the human boat to earth, that it may sail on smoother seas... —*Matheno*

Death? Translated into the heavenly tongue, that word means life... —*Henry W. Beecher*

To meet death not only as an event at the end of life but as an ever–present ingredient in the life process itself is the final goal to be sought... —*J. Bruce Long*

Death is not a foe, but an inevitable adventure...
—*Oliver Lodge*

After your death you will be what you were before your birth...
—*Arthur Schopenhauer*

We should weep for men at their birth, not at their death...
—*Baron de Montesquieu*

We understand death for the first time when he puts his hand upon one whom we love... —*Madame de Staël*

There is no death. They only truly live who pass into the life beyond, and see this earth as but a school preparative for higher ministry... —*John Oxenham*

Nature invented death that there might be new life...
—Johann W. Goethe

On the day of his death, a man feels he has lived but a single day...
—The Zohar

Death, so called, is a thing which makes men weep, and yet a third of life is passed in sleep...
—George Byron

Death is the greatest of all human blessings...
—Plato

It is only in the face of death that man's self is born...
—Augustine

People fear death because what happens at death is unknown. However...I look forward to the change called death as life's last great adventure...
—Peace Pilgrim

What better can the Lord do for man than take him home when he has done his work?...
—Charles Kingsley

The fear of death keeps us from living, not from dying...
—Paul Roud

Death is a punishment to some, to some a gift, and to many a favor...
—Seneca

What is death? A mask. Turn it and be convinced. See, it does not bite...
—Epicteus

Death is not a period but a comma in the story of life...
—Amos J. Traver

Death for those who understand it is immortality, but for those unenlightened ones, who do not understand it, it is death...
—St. Antony, the Great

It is not hard to die. It is harder, a thousand times harder, to live...
—Henry W. Beecher

Alas for those who never sing but die with all their music in them...
—Oliver W. Holmes

A dying man needs to die as a sleeping man needs to sleep, and there comes a time when it is wrong, as well as useless, to resist... —*Stewart Alsop*

Don't be afraid your life will end; be afraid it will never begin... —*Grace Hanson*

Death is a debt we all must pay... —*Euripides*

Death, when it approaches, ought not to take one by surprise. It should be part of the full expectancy of life... —*Muriel Spark*

Weep not for him who departs from life, for there is no suffering beyond death... —*Palladas*

We weep when we are born, not when we die!... —*Thomas B. Aldrich*

The end of birth is death; the end of death is birth; this is ordained... —*Edwin Arnold*

If life must not be taken too seriously - then so neither must death... —*Samuel Butler*

Death is experienced only once; but he who fears it dies each minute... —*Solomon Rubin*

Death is just a distant rumor to the young... —*Andy Rooney*

Are you afraid you don't know how to die? Don't worry. Nature will take care of that for you... —*Marco Vassi*

As soon as a man comes to life, he is immediately old enough to die... —*Der Ackermon aus Böhmen*

Whoever is interested in life is particularly interested in death... —*Thomas Mann*

Death is but a sharp corner near the beginning of life's procession down eternity... —*Ayscough*

Dying is a wild night and a new road....*(night of death)*
—*Emily Dickinson*

If I had the strength to hold a pen, I would write down how easy and pleased it is to die... —*William Hunter*

Depression/Despair

The attitude of unhappiness is not only painful, it is mean and ugly... —*William James*

Unhappiness is best defined as the difference between our talents and our expectations... —*Edward de Bono*

It is ironic that man should feel such a painful void inside of himself when he lives in a world of so many things...but which apparently cannot fill the heart... —*John Powell*

Men who are unhappy, like men who sleep badly, are always proud of the fact... —*Bertrand Russell*

Don't let life discourage you: everyone who got where he is had to begin where he was... —*Richard Evans*

Depression is a disorder of mood, so mysteriously painful and elusive...as to verge close to being beyond description...
—*William Styron*

Noble deeds and hot baths are the best cures for depression... —*Dodie Smith*

Helplessness leads to panic, and panic leads to depression...
—*Martin E.P. Seligman*

Depression occurs when you are not being yourself. You're probably doing things you don't want to do... —*Eda LeShan*

Depression is the inability to construct a future...
—*Rollo May*

When I am depressed, somewhere deep inside, I know that I am denying the presence of God... —*Gerald Jampolsky*

Sadness usually results from one of the following causes–either when a man does not succeed, or is ashamed of his success... *—Seneca*

We are unhappy only when we want things other than they are... *—Lucy Cornellssen*

Despair is the damp of hell, as joy is the serenity of heaven... *—John Donne*

To be melancholy is to be forever thinking of oneself... *—Comtesse Diane*

Never despair, but if you do, work on in despair... *—Edmund Burke*

One must never despair if something is lost to one, a person or a joy or a happiness; everything comes back again more gloriously... *—Rainer M. Rilke*

Sometimes sadness and sorrow wash the eyes with the tears of a more perfect understanding... *—Fred Van Amburgh*

Sorrows are like thunderclouds. Far off they look black, but directly over us merely gray... *—Jean Paul Richter*

When a person drowns himself in negative thinking he is committing an unspeakable crime against himself... *—Maxwell Maltz*

The great enemy of the soul is not trial but sadness, which is the bleeding wound of self love... *—William B. Villathorne*

In depression we look for evidence of anger behind the saddened aspect... *—Albert Rothenberg*

The best thing for being sad is to learn something... *—T.H. White*

What we call despair is often only the painful eagerness of unfed hope... *—George Eliot*

Melancholy is a symptom of on-coming sickness...
—*Nahman Bratzlav*

Despair is the absolute extreme of self love...
—*Thomas Merton*

Desire

Want is a growing giant whom the coat of have was never large enough to cover... —*Ralph W. Emerson*

Every attachment is a sign of our insuficiency...A truly happy being is a solitary being... —*Jean J. Rousseau*

The deepest human urge is the desire to be important...
—*John Dewey*

Desire blinds us, like the pickpocket who sees only the saint's pockets... —*Jack Kornfield*

Wherever there is desire, association with it brings endless misery... —*Gampopa*

If thou will make a man happy, add not unto his riches but take away from his desires... —*Epicurus*

The discipline of desire is the background of character...
—*John Locke*

Impossible desires are punished in the desire...
—*Philip Sidney*

Destiny has two ways of crushing us— by refusing our wishes and by fulfilling them... —*Henri F. Amiel*

My belief is that to have no wants is divine... —*Socrates*

The marvelous things about human beings is that we are perpetually reaching for the stars. The more we have, the more we want. And for this reason, we never have it all...
—*Joyce Brothers*

Other desires perish in their gratification, but the desire of knowledge never... —*Alfred E. Housman*

When all desire is surrendered but the desire to function as God wills, the way is opened before you...
—*Amy & Evarts Loomis*

Our desires always disappoint us; for though we meet with something that gives us satisfaction, yet it never thoroughly answers our expectations... —*Francois La Rochefoucauld*

Desires are like a forest fire...consuming and destroying everything... —*Philo*

Every desire is insatiable, and therefore is always in want...
—*Sextus, the Pythogorean*

Who clings faithfully to God desires nothing for himself...
—*Itzikl of Radvil*

It is difficult to overcome one's passions, and it is impossible to satisfy them... —*Marguerite De la Sabiere*

If you did not desire your present position, you would not be doing everything possible to maintain it... —*Leo Tolstoy*

A life is either all spiritual or not spiritual at all. No man can serve two masters. Your life is shaped by the end you live for. You are made in the image of what you desire...
—*Thomas Merton*

When desire is quenched, peace is found... —*Paul Brunton*

It is better to desire the things we have than to have the things we desire... —*Henry Van Dyke*

The thirst of desire is never filled, nor fully satisfied...
—*Cicero*

It is much easier to suppress a first desire than to satisfy those that follow... —*Francois La Rochefoucauld*

It is with our passions, as it is with fire and water, they are good servants but bad masters... —*Roger L'Estrange*

Covetousness is the root of all evil, the ground of all vice... —*Leonard Wright*

Desire grows in strength if you follow it, but dies if you turn from it and abstain...Desire is slavery; renunciation is freedom... —*Hermes*

We would often be sorry if our wishes were granted... —*Aesop*

When the gods want to punish us, they grant our desires... —*Ancient Greek saying*

It is not good to be too free. It is not good to have everything one wants... —*Blaise Pascal*

Devil

The devil is an egotist... —*Johann W. Goethe*

It is no good casting out devils. They belong to us and we must accept them and be at peace with them... —*D.H. Lawrence*

The only devil from which men must be redeemed is self, the lower self. If man would find his devil he must look within; his name is self... —*The Aquarian Gospel*

If the devil does not exist, and man has therefore created him, he has created him in his own image and likeness... —*Fyodor Dostoyevsky*

God is good, there is no devil but fear; nothing can harm us, the Universe is planned for our good... —*Elbert Hubbard*

When the devil is called the God of this world, it is not because he made it, but because we serve him with our worldliness.. —*Thomas Aquinas*

The only real devil that exists in this or any other world is the man whose business is that of making devils...

—*Napoleon Hill*

The devil is in whatever tries to master you. If you do not resist, he will temporarily master you...Resist the devil and he will flee from you... —*Prentice Mulford*

Stand up to the devil and he will turn and run. Come close to God and God will come close to you... —*New Testament*

Discipline

If you have mastered yourself, nature will obey you...

—*Eliphas Levi*

When you learn to discipline your mind, you become master of your mind rather than your mind being master of you... —*Ormond McGill*

What makes a man a good artist, a good sculptor, a good musician? Practice. What makes a man a good linguist, a good stenographer? Practice. What makes a man a good man? Practice. Nothing else... —*Henry Drummond*

He who cannot obey himself will be commanded. This is the nature of living creatures... —*Friedrich W. Nietzsche*

The only worthy discipline is self discipline... —*Wayne Dyer*

If you cannot command your own soul, how can I give you enlightenment how to do so?... —*Marjorie Bowen*

The man who refuses to submit to discipline is like a river that overflows its banks, thereby destroying the means by which it could reach the sea...Fortunately, it is not left entirely to us to discipline ourselves. Life does it for us...

—*Alice H. Rice*

Self-discipline does within while you do without...

—*Denis Waitley*

Most powerful is he who has himself in his own power...
—Seneca

The difference between a savior and a sinner is this: that the one has perfect control of all the forces within him; the other is dominated and controlled by them...
—James Allen

No man is free who cannot command himself...
—Pythagoras

Self-discipline is your golden key; without it, you cannot be happy... *—Maxwell Maltz*

Self-conquest is the greatest of victories... *—Plato*

He that cannot decidedly say "No" when tempted to evil is on the highway to ruin... *—Joel Hawes*

Without consistency there is no moral strength...
—John J. Owen

There never has been, and cannot be, a good life without self control; apart from self control, no good life is imaginable... *—Herbert Spencer*

One must train oneself, by small and frequent efforts, to dominate one's feelings... *—Alexis Carrel*

He who reigns within himself and rules his passions, desires and fears is more than a king... *—John Milton*

Above everything, you must command yourself, and your true self is not your wildly roving thoughts...
—Berthold Auerbach

Self-knowledge and self-improvement are very difficult for most people. It usually needs great courage and long struggle... *—Abraham Maslow*

If you would learn self-mastery, begin by yielding yourself to the One Great Master... *—Johann Lobstein*

Our own inner child has to be disciplined in order to release its tremendous spiritual power... —*Marion Woodman*

Self-control may be developed, precisely the same manner as we tone up a weak muscle—by little exercises day by day... —*W.G. Jordan*

It is one thing to praise discipline, and another thing to submit to it... —*Miguel de Cervantes*

The virtue of all achievement is victory over oneself. Those who know this victory can never know defeat... —*A.J. Cronin*

Cheerfulness is the rich and satisfying result of strenuous discipline... —*Edwin P. Whipple*

Man has six organs to serve him, and he is master only of three. He cannot control his eye, ear or nose, but he can his mouth, hand and foot... —*Amora Levi*

There never has been, and cannot be, a good life without self control... —*Leo Tolstoy*

Whoever preaches absence of discipline is an enemy of progress... —*Max Nordau*

Exercise, exercise your powers; what is difficult will finally become routine... —*George C. Lichtenberg*

No one is free who is not master of himself... —*William Shakespeare*

Doubt

Despair is an expression of the total personality, doubt only of thought... —*Sören Kierkegaard*

Doubt is really a groping ignorance... —*Eliphas Levi*

Hidden doubts and fears build walls around you... —*Paul Williams*

God gave us faith. The devil introduced doubt...
—Fred Van Amburgh

Doubts are more cruel than the worst of truths...
—Jean B. Moliere

Doubt is brother devil to despair... *—John B. O'Reilly*

Skepticism is slow suicide...Skepticism is unbelief in cause and effect... *—Ralph W. Emerson*

Doubt of whatever kind, can be ended by Action alone...
—Thomas Carlyle

Doubt is not a pleasant condition, but certainty is an absurd one... *—Voltaire*

Doubt grows with knowledge... *—Johann W. Goethe*

The end of doubt is the beginning of repose... *—Petrarch*

Doubt indulged soon becomes doubt realized...
—Francis R. Havergal

Where doubt is, there truth is—it is her shadow...
—Gamaliel Bailey

It is only by doubting that we eventually come to the truth...
—Cicero

A fanatic is a man who consciously overcompensates a secret doubt... *—Aldous Huxley*

If you would be a real seeker of the truth, it is necessary at least once in your life to doubt, as far as possible, all things...
—Rene Descartes

With most people, doubt about one thing is simply blind belief in another... *—George C. Lichtenberg*

Doubt comes in the window when inquiry is denied at the door... *—Benjamin Jowett*

Doubt is the beginning, not the end of wisdom...

—*George Ileo*

When you are in doubt, be still, and wait. When doubt no longer exists for you, then go forward in courage...

—*White Eagle*

As long as there is a material body, you are carrying doubt. Do not despise your doubting. That is the human condition. When there is no more doubt, you do not need to be human... —*Emmanuel*

Dreams

Dream delivers us to dream and there is no end to illusion...

—*Ralph W. Emerson*

If a man advances confidently in the direction of his dreams to live the life he has imagined, he will meet with success unexpected in common hours... —*Henry D. Thoreau*

Hold fast to dreams for if dreams die, life is a broken-winged bird that cannot fly... —*Langston Hughes*

Within our dreams and aspirations we find our opportunities... —*Sue A. Ebaugh*

Dream lofty dreams, and as you dream, so shall you become. Your vision is the promise of what you shall one day be, your ideal is the prophecy of what you shall at last unveil...

—*James Allen*

Dreams are so important in one's life, yet when followed blindly they can lead to the disintegration of the soul...

—*Maria Campbell*

It can be a very dangerous thing to go in search of a dream for the reality does not always match it... —*Gracie Fields*

We grow through our dreams. All great men and women are dreamers... —*Woodrow Wilson*

Have a dream and believe in it. Strong dreams always come true... *—Robert Muller*

High on the wall, in the castle of your dreams of success, hangs the picture of what you want to be. Always keep that picture hanging there. See yourself where you intend to be. Night and day dream of what you intend to do and what you intend to be, for your dreams interpret your intentions always. All successes are, at first, dreams...
—Fred Van Amburgh

If you can dream it, you can do it... *—Walt Disney*

The greatest achievement was at first and for a time a dream. The oak sleeps in the acorn; the bird waits in the egg; and in the highest vision of the soul, a waking angel stirs. Dreams are the seedling of realities... *—James Allen*

If you can imagine it, you can achieve it. If you can dream it, you can become it... *—William A. Ward*

Waiting and hoping are the whole of life, and as soon as a dream is realized it is destroyed... *—Giancarlo Menotti*

When your heart's dream becomes a burning desire to achieve and accomplish its specific purpose, the entire cosmos opens its doors to you... *—Lloyd Littlepage*

Take time to dream—it is hitching your wagon to a star...
—Irish prayer

Existence would be intolerable if we were never to dream...
—Antole France

All that we see or seem is but a dream within a dream...
—Edgar A. Poe

All men dream - but not equally. Those who dream by night in the dusty recesses of their minds wake in the day to find it was vanity: but the dreamers of the day are dangerous men, for they may act their dreams with open eyes, to make it possible... —*T.E. Lawrence*

Nothing happens unless first a dream... —*Carl Sandburg*

Dreaming is an act of pure imagination, attesting in all men a creative power... —*Frederick H. Hedge*

Waking life is a dream controlled... —*George Santayana*

Dream big dreams, then put on your overalls and go out and make the dreams come true... —*Fred Van Amburgh*

Dreams are the touchstones of our character...
—*Henry D. Thoreau*

The dreamers are the saviors of the world. As the visible world is sustained by the invisible, so men, through all their trials and sins and sordid vocations, are nourished by the visions of their solitary dreamers... —*James Allen*

Kill a dream and the dreamer dies too... —*Leonard M. Foley*

Duality

People wish to swim and at the same time keep one foot on the ground... —*Marcel Proust*

Joy is at its keenest when contrasted with sorrow, courage at its height when it follows fear, faith at its noblest when it grows from doubt... —*Alice H. Rice*

Each of us can feel a dual life within ourselves. The struggle of the mind against the conscience; of unmanly desire against noble feelings; in a word, of the brute against the intelligent creature... —*Eliphas Levi*

There is no fruit which is not bitter before it is ripe...
—*Publilius Syrus*

Where there is much light, the shadow is deep...
—*Johann W. Goethe*

To the man of God right and wrong are alike...
—Divani Shamsi Tabriz

Everything is plain and easy to the earnest; it is the double-minded who find difficulties... *—John H. Newman*

Two men look out through the same bars; one sees the mud, and one the stars... *—Frederick Langbridge*

As long as you are concerned about what you do, that is dualistic... *—Shunryu Suzuki*

Every man, in reality, is two men. The man he is, and the man he could be... *—Earl Nightingale*

The masters say that the soul has two faces. The higher one always sees God, the lower one looks downward and informs the senses... *—Meister Eckhart*

There are two souls in my own breast, and one is determined to beat down the other... *—Johann W. Goethe*

For everything you have missed, you have gained something else; and for everything you gain, you lose something...
—Ralph W. Emerson

Ego/Vanity

To be egotistic is to be blind to the needs, and the reality, of others... *—Robert Mueller*

Your ego is an event and not a thing, and it is in a continual state of flux; it changes a thousand times each day and takes a thousand forms... *—Ormond McGill*

All pruning of the ego is of little use, for as one fault is removed a new one springs out of latency... *—Paul Brunton*

Flattery is counterfeit money which, but for vanity, would have no circulation... *—Francois La Rochefoucauld*

One may understand the cosmos, but never the ego; the

self is more distant than any star... —*G.K. Chesterton*

Self centeredness...takes two forms; Thinking too well of one's self and thinking too ill...It is harder to cure the latter than the former... —*Alice H. Rice*

The problem is that the ego can convert anything to its own use, even spirituality. Ego is constantly attempting to acquire and apply the teachings of spirituality for its own benefit...
—*Chögyam Trungpa*

Intrinsically, there is no ego—it is something that we ourselves create... —*Roshi P. Kapleau*

Self realization is the great goal of living, but where the ego is, realization is not... —*Robert S. Ellwood*

To sum up all in a word: Nothing has separated us from God but our own will, or rather our own will is our separation from God... —*William Law*

Let no one think he has been appointed the Savior...
—*Johann W. Goethe*

Half of the harm that is done in the world is due to people who want to feel important... —*T.S. Eliot*

The ego has the power of making imaginative forms which can be used in the world of purification or made...to magnify fears, passions and powers... —*Ray Mitchell*

Egotism erects its center in itself; love places it out of itself in the axis of the universal whole... —*Friedrich von Schiller*

When a man is wrapped up in himself he makes a pretty small package... —*John Ruskin*

Of all the foolish vices, vanity is the foolishest...
—*Fred Van Amburgh*

We do not content ourselves with the life we have in ourselves; we desire to live an imaginary life in the minds of others, and for this purpose we endeavor to shine...

—Blaise Pascal

Just about the most useless desire we can have is the desire to impress other people... *—Vernon Howard*

The most overrated thing in the world is your opinion of yourself...the more you think yourself spiritual...the more the ego deflates itself... *—Raymond C. Barker*

Intolerance itself is a form of egoism, and to condemn egoism intolerantly is to share it... *—George Santayana*

We are so vain that we even care for the opinion of those we don't care for... *—Marie Von Ebner–Eschenbach*

The way of the ego is to have us forget about God by getting and attaching ourselves to people and things...

—Gerald Jampolsky

The ego frightens us in innumerable ways: with death, with pain, with loneliness... *—Lily Benatar*

Keep God in remembrance until your self is forgotten...

—Shams Tabriz

Egotism: the art of seeing in yourself what others cannot see... *—George Higgins*

The root of all discontent is self love... *—James F. Clarke*

Man seeks something which will give him a brief moment of satisfaction; and his ego will often follow the most tortuous paths to obtain this moment... *—Hans–Ulrick Rieker*

The great corrupter of public man is the ego...Looking at the mirror distracts one's attention from the problem...

—Dean Acheson

He that falls in love with himself will have no rivals...

—Benjamin Franklin

It is a curious fact that of all the illusions that beset mankind, none is quite so curious as that tendency to suppose that we are mentally and morally superior to those who differ from us in opinion... —*Elbert Hubbard*

There is nothing contrary to God in the whole world, nothing that fights against him, but self will...
—*Ralph Cudworth*

The best way of seeing divine light is to put out your own little candle... —*English proverb*

The ego will always be able to find ways to keep the aspirant busy in self improvement, thus binding him to the fact that the self is still there behind all improvements. For why should the ego kill itself?... —*Paul Brunton*

An egotist will always speak of himself, either in praise or censure; but the modest man ever shuns making himself the subject of his conversation... —*Jean La Bruyere*

The fullest possible enjoyment is to be found by reducing your ego to zero... —*G.K. Chesterton*

When the ego life dissolves and dies in silence, then one lives the life supreme of pure awareness... —*Vachaka Kovia*

Emotions

The emotions may be endless. The more we express them, the more we may have to express... —*E.M. Forster*

Many worthy causes have been lost because they were founded on emotion instead of facts...
—*Whitney S. Seymour, Jr.*

Since emotions are few and reasons are many, the behavior of a crowd can be more easily predicted than the behavior of one person can... —*Isaac Asimov*

Our emotions can take us to God or they can take us to hell... —*Alan Cohen*

Thought is deeper than all speech, feeling deeper than all thought... —*Christopher Cranch*

Good emotions are the best medicine... —*John A. Schindler*

Emotions should be servants, not masters—or at least not tyrants... —*Robert Benson*

We have lost confidence in reason because we have learned that man is chiefly a creature of habit and emotion... —*John Dewey*

The taste for emotion may become a dangerous taste; we should be very cautious how we attempt to squeeze out of human life more ecstasy and paroxysm than it can well afford... —*Sidney Smith*

We are all human beings. We have emotions. Men and women just express them differently. That is the difference between us. Women want to talk about their emotions, whereas men want to privately deal with them and think them through... —*John Gray*

To be calm and well poised is to be the center of power. The weak are those who have no control of their feelings and emotions... —*Leon DeSeblo*

Passion of any kind is a bad counselor... —*Paul Brunton*

The strongest and most fantastic fact about negative emotions is that people actually worship them... —*P.D. Ouspensky*

Emotions...become more violent when expression is stilted... —*Philo*

When a man is prey to his emotions, he is not his master... —*Baruch Spinoza*

If negative emotions produce negative chemical changes in the body, wouldn't the positive emotions produce positive chemical changes?... —*Norman Cousins*

All emotions are pure which gather you and lift you up; that emotion is impure which seizes only one side of your being and so distorts you... *—Rainer M. Rilke*

Emotion which does not lead to and flow out in right action is not only useless, but it weakens character, and becomes an excuse for neglect of effort... *—Tryon Edwards*

Emotions are color of life; we would be drab creatures indeed without them. But we must control these emotions or they will control us... *—John M. Wilson*

Enemy

One of the most time consuming things is to have an enemy... *—E.B. White*

Man is wise...when he recognizes no greater enemy than himself... *—Marguerite of Navarre*

It is hard to fight an enemy who has outposts in your head... *—Sally Kempton*

It pays to know the enemy—not the least because at some time you may have the opportunity to turn him into a friend... *—Margaret Thatcher*

Build your adversary a golden bridge over which to retreat... *—Sun Tzu*

If we could reach the secret history of our enemies we shall find in each man's sorrow and suffering enough to disarm all hostility... *—Henry W. Longfellow*

No one is to be called an enemy; all are your benefactors, and no one does you harm. You have no enemy except yourselves... *—Francis of Assisi*

Our only enemies are those inside ourselves. They are our weaknesses and vices, our lower passions and intellectual deformities. It is better to fight them than other men... *—Paul Brunton*

The most discouraging, destroying and wretched enemies that can exist...are negative thoughts...—*Fred Van Amburgh*

Our enemies are our outward consciences...
—*William Shakespeare*

Never disregard what your enemies say. They may be severe, they may be prejudiced, they may be determined to see only in one direction, but still in that direction they see clearly. They do not speak all the truth, but they generally speak the turth from one point of view; so far as that goes, attend to them... —*Benjamin Haydon*

Better a thousand enemies outside the house than one inside... —*Arabian proverb*

We should never make enemies, if for no other reason, because it is so hard to behave toward them as we ought...
—*Ray Palmer*

A wise man gets more use from his enemies than a fool from his friends... —*Baltasar Gracian*

Man's chief enemy is his own unruly nature and the dark forces pent up within him... —*Earnest Jones*

Beware of no man more than yourself; we carry our worst enemies within us... —*Charles H. Spurgeon*

Men of sense often learn from their enemies...—*Aristophanes*

Love your enemies, bless them that curse you, do good to them that hate you, and pray for them which spitefully use you and persecute you... —*Jesus*

Pay attention to your enemies, for they are the first to discover your mistakes... —*Antishenes*

If you want enemies, excel others; if friends, let others excel you... —*Charles C. Colton*

In order to have an enemy, one must be somebody...
—*Ann S. Swetchine*

Everyone is his own enemy... —*St. Bernard*

Those who hate you don't win unless you hate them and then you destroy yourself... —*Richard M. Nixon*

Energy

Creative words generate energy; negative words drain out energy... —*Robert Schuller*

The body is consuming energy when tense and restoring energy when it is relaxed... —*John Lust*

There is no genius in life like the genius of energy... —*Donald G. Mitchell*

Energy can do anything that can be done in the world... —*Johann W. Goethe*

Love the moment, and the energy of that moment will spread out beyond all boundaries... —*Corita Kent*

He alone has energy who cannot be deprived of it... —*John K. Lavater*

Recharging ourselves with endless energy is accomplished simply by consciously thinking of those qualities we know as joy, happiness, enthusiasm, inspiration and ecstasy... —*Cheryl Canfield*

Cosmic energy enters any man who will receive it. It flows into his every action, transforming all he touches. But it cannot come in save as it flows out... —*Dave Seabury*

The most exhausting thing in life is being insincere. This is why so much social life is exhausting... —*Anne Morrow Lindbergh*

The universe is energy that responds to expectations... —*James Redfield*

Once we open up to the flow of energy within our body, we also open up to the flow of the energy in the universe...
—*Wilhelm Reich*

Enlightenment

There is no difference between an enlightened man and an ignorant one. What makes the difference, is that the one realizes it, while the other is kept in ignorance of it...
—*Hui Neng*

Enlightenment is "being", and it grows; its end is serenity...
—*William Gibson*

Enlightenment is the natural condition of life after you strip the unnatural heavy and dark conditions away...
—*Ron Smothermon*

If you are enlightened, you are not free, as some people say, but you are freedom itself. Not like a bird in the sky, but like the sky itself...
—*Walter A. Keers*

Since I received enlightenment in the infinite wonders of truth I have always been cheerful and laughing...
—*Hung Chou*

If a man is free from sin, his mind and heart must be opened to the influence of enlightenment...
—*The Talmud*

Enlightenment is not an attainment; it is a realization. When you wake up, everything changes and nothing changes. If a blind man realizes that he can see, has the world changed?...
—*Dan Millman*

The attainment of enlightenment from ego's point of view is extreme death...
—*Chögyam Trungpa*

Enthusiasm

Enthusiasm is the greatest asset in the world. It is nothing more or less than faith in action...
—*Henry Chester*

Enthusiasm is not a thing which some possess and others lack. All persons have it potentially, but only a few are able to express it... —*William W. Atkinson*

Enthusiasm changes the quality of the job because it changes people... —*Norman V. Peale*

Look at everything as though you were seeing it for the first or last time. Then your time on earth will be filled with glory... —*Betty Smith*

If we find nothing of interest where we are, we are likely to find little of lasting interest where we wish to go... —*Edwin W. Teale*

Enthusiasm is the temper of the mind in which the imagination has got the better of judgement... —*William Warburton*

When a man's willing and eager, God joins in...—*Aeschylus*

Your enthusiasm is not dead; it merely hides below your cynical practicality... —*David Seabury*

Enthusiasm is the genius of sincerity; and truth accomplishes no victories without it.... —*Edward Bulwer–Lytton*

Enthusiasm gives life to what is invisible...—*Madame de Staël*

Great designs are not accomplished without enthusiasm of some sort. It is the inspiration of everything great... —*Christian Bovee*

Enthusiasm is the father of excellence... —*Bruce A. Johnson*

If you can give your son or daughter only one gift, let it be enthusiasm... —*Bruce Barton*

The worst bankrupt is the person who has lost enthusiasm. Let one lose everything but enthusiasm and that person will again come through to success... —*H.W. Arnold*

Opposition always inflames the enthusiast, never converts him... —*Johann von Schiller*

A man without judgement is like a car without brakes, but a man without enthusiasm is like a car without a motor... — *Judith Lane*

None are so old as those who have outlived enthusiasm... —*Henry D. Thoreau*

Enthusiasm is one of life's greatest qualities, but it must be practiced to become a dominant factor in one's life...There is real magic in enthusiasm. It spells the difference between mediocrity and accomplishment... —*Norman V. Peale*

Envy/Jealousy

When envy consumes us, we are unable to love, unable to appreciate others. Envy opens the floodgates to our darkest emotions and our most mean–spirited inclinations... —*Melvyn Kinder*

Jealousy, that dragon that slays love under the pretense of keeping it alive... —*Havelock Ellis*

Nothing is more capable of troubling our reason and consuming our health, than secret notions of jealousy in solitude... —*Aphra Behir*

To jealousy, nothing is more frightful than laughter... —*Francoise Sagan*

Jealousy is indeed a poor medium to secure love, but it is a secure medium to destroy one's self-respect... —*Emma Goldman*

When men are full of envy they disparage everything, whether it be good or bad... —*Tacitus*

Jealousy lives upon doubts. It becomes madness or ceases entirely as soon as we pass from doubt to certainty... —*Francois La Rochefoucauld*

Envy shooteth at others, but hitteth and woundeth herself...
—*Gabriel Harvey*

Jealousy is more self-love than love...
—*Francois La Rochefoucauld*

Envy has a thousand eyes, but none with correct vision...
—*Issachar Hurwitz*

It would be an error to try to build the Kingdom of Heaven upon envy. For nothing that is founded on envy can thrive; it must have another root... —*Paracelsus*

Jealousy is the fear or apprehension of superiority; envy, our uneasiness under it... —*William Shenstone*

Envy requires keeping your eyes off yourself and focused on others... —*Melvyn Kinder*

Evil

Good is great and real; hence, its opposite, evil, must be small and unreal... —*Mary Baker Eddy*

Evil is merely a mask—a dysfunction... —*Wendy Kaminer*

Nothing which is naturally inevitable can possibly be evil. Winter, night, death are not evils. They are the natural transitions from one day to another day, from autumn to spring, from one life to another life... —*Eliphas Levi*

The evil you know is better than the evil you don't know...
—*Russian proverb*

Sin and evil are nothing less than our inability to love...
—*Thomas M. MacDonald*

The belief in a supernatural power of evil is not necessary; men alone are quite capable of every wickedness...
—*Joseph Conrad*

If evil existed, this would mean God created it. Such a thing is impossible. If there were two equal powers, they would neutralize each other. What we see as evil is not ultimately real but is simply a result of the creative power of thought...
—Shirley Briggs

There is only one good—knowledge, and one evil—ignorance... *—Socrates*

For as long as the root of wickedness is hidden, it is strong but when it is recognized it is dissolved... *—Gospel of Phillip*

There is a great difference between resisting the negative force and renouncing it. When you resist this dark force, or what man calls evil, you give the subject attention and growth. When you renounce evil you take your attention from it and give your attention to what you want... *—Darwin Gross*

In the huge mass of evil as it rolls and swells, there is ever some good working toward deliverance and triumph...
—Thomas Carlyle

The only evil there is, is the belief in a self hood or a condition separate and apart from God... *—Joel Goldsmith*

The first way to avoid an evil, is to know it, and to know the cause and occasion of it... *—Benjamin Whichcote*

Good has but one enemy, the evil; but the evil has two enemies, the good and itself... *—Johannes von Muller*

The exit of evil works the entrance of virtue... *—Philo*

The basic formula for all sin is: frustrated or neglected love...
—Franz Werfel

It is not sufficient to deny or ignore evil; it must be understood. It is not enough to pray to God to remove the evil; you must find out why it is there, and what lesson it has for you. It is of no avail to fret and fume and chafe at the chains that bind you; you must know how and why you are bound...
— James Allen

Without evil the all would be incomplete. For most or even all forms of evil serve the Universe...Vice itself has many useful sides... —*Plotinus*

Evil is like poison ivy; the more you scratch, the more it itches, and the more it spreads... —*A. Nicolas*

Evil is not being, it is a hole in being, a lack. That is why there can be no absolute evil... —*Yves M. Congar*

Evil is neither person, place, nor being, but simply a belief, an illusion of material sense... —*Mary Baker Eddy*

Example

Few things are harder to put up with than the annoyance of a good example... —*Mark Twain*

Be a pattern to others, and all will go well: for as a whole city is affected by the promiscuous passions of great men, so it is likewise reformed by their moderation... —*Cicero*

People never improve unless they look to some standard or example higher and better than themselves...
—*Tryon Edwards*

Nothing is so infectious as example... —*Charles Kingsley*

Live with wolves and you will soon learn to howl...
—*Spanish proverb*

Precept is instruction written in the sand. The tide flows over it, and the record is gone. Example is graven on the rock, and the lesson is not soon lost...
—*William E. Channing*

My advice is to consult the lives of other men, as one would a looking glass, and from thence fetch examples for imitation... —*Terence*

Children have never been very good at listening to their elders, but they have never failed to imitate them...
—*James Baldwin*

None preach better than the ant, and she says nothing...
—*Benjamin Franklin*

No reproof or denunciation is so perfect as the silent influence of a good example... —*Maturin Ballou*

Example is the school of mankind, and they will learn at no other... —*Edmund Burke*

People seldom improve when they have no model but themselves to copy after... —*Oliver Goldsmith*

I have ever deemed it more honorable and more profitable, too, to set a good example than to follow a bad one...
—*Thomas Jefferson*

Do not take the example of another as an excuse for your wrongdoing... —*Eknath Easwaran*

Example is a lesson that all men can read... —*Gilbert West*

The only rational way of education is to be an example—if you can't help it, a warning example... —*Albert Einstein*

One example is more valuable...than twenty precepts written in books... —*Roger Ascham*

Make small commitments and keep them. Be a light, not a judge. Be a model, not a critic. Be part of the solution, not part of the problem... —*Stephen R. Covey*

He who lives well is the best preacher...
—*Miguel de Cervantes*

Example is not the main thing in influencing others. It is the only thing... —*Albert Schweitzer*

Failure/Mistake

Faliure will never overtake you if your determination to succeed is strong enough... —*Og Mandino*

Thinking like a winner means not always having to defeat someone else. It means being able to grow from a situation in which you fail to meet your goal... —*Wayne Dyer*

The only failure a man ought to fear is failure to cleaving to the purpose he sees to be best... —*George Eliot*

A series of failures may culminate in the best possible result... —*Gisela Richter*

To understand how something works, it helps to know how it can fail... —*Marvin Minsky*

Defeat is a school in which truth always grows strong... —*Henry W. Beecher*

You only fail if you quit trying... —*Edgar Cayce*

If you can learn to learn from failure, you'll go pretty much where you want to go... —*Arthur Gordon*

Failure is often God's own tool for carving some of the finest outlines in the character of his children... —*Thomas Hodgkin*

Failure is instructive. The person who really thinks, learns quite as much from his failures as from his successes... —*John Dewey*

Failures are divided into two classes—those who thought and never did, and those who did and never thought... —*John C. Salak*

In God's economy, nothing is wasted. Through failure, we learn a lesson in humility which is probably needed, painful though it is... —*Bill Wilson*

Through humiliation and despair, failure and mistakes, the ego may be crushed to the ground... —*Paul Brunton*

You always pass failure on the way to success... —*Mickey Rooney*

Failures always overtake those who have the power to do, without the will to act... —*James Ellis*

There is no cure for failure, except success; it is failure that gives success its value... —*Walter Winchell*

Defeat never comes to any man until he admits it...
—*Josephus Daniels*

Failures come to all of us. No matter how hard we try sometimes, things will go wrong...Do not be discouraged because of failures; begin over... —*Ida S. Taylor*

We learn wisdom from failure much more than from success. We often discover what will do by finding out what will not do, and probably he who never made a mistake never made a discovery... —*Samuel Smiles*

Failure is just another word for learning...failure can lead us in new directions... —*Lois Wolfe-Morgan*

Failure is only postponed success... —*Herbert Kaufman*

I cannot give you a formula for success, but I can give you the formula for failure—which is: try to please everybody...
—*Herbert B. Swope*

The biggest contributor to failure is a poor self image...
—*Will Munson*

Strong people make as many and as ghastly mistakes as weak people. The difference is that strong people admit them, laugh at them, learn from them. This is how they become strong... —*Richard Needham*

Good people are good because they've come to wisdom through failure... —*William Saroyan*

There is always another chance...This thing called "failure" is not the falling down but staying down... —*Mary Pickford*

Any man may make a mistake, but none but the fool will continue in it... —*Cicero*

Every great mistake has a halfway moment, a split second when it can be recalled and perhaps remedied...

—*Pearl Buck*

Of course we make mistakes; it's how we learn. We're all in training. Life can be difficult; what an opportunity...

—*Dan Millman*

No persons are more frequently wrong, than those who will not admit they are wrong... —*Francois La Rochefoucauld*

The only man who never makes a mistake is the man who never does anything... —*Theodore Roosevelt*

Failure is the opportunity to begin again more intelligently...

—*Henry Ford*

A man carries his success or failure with him: it is not dependent upon outside conditions... —*Ralph W. Trine*

Faith

All the strength and force of man comes from his faith in things unseen... —*J.F. Clarke*

Faith receives; love gives. No one will be able to receive without faith. No one will be able to give without love...

—*Gospel of Philip*

The principal part of faith is patience...—*Goerge MacDonald*

One doesn't discover new lands without consenting to lose sight of the shore for a very long time... —*André Gide*

If you have faith as a grain of a mustard seed, you shall say unto the mountain, "Remove hence to yonder place," and it shall remove and nothing will be impossible to you...

—*Jesus*

Faith begins as an experiment and ends as an experience...
—*W.R. Inge*

It is necessary to the happiness of man that he be mentally faithful to himself... —*Thomas Paine*

Fear knocked at the door. Faith answered... —*Irish proverb*

Faith is a simple childlike belief in a Divine Friend who solves all problems that come to us... —*Helen Keller*

When proof is possible, faith becomes impossible! And when proof is impossible, faith becomes possible!...
—*Robert Schuller*

In the midst of winter I found within me an invincible summer... —*Albert Camus*

If you have faith in God, or man, or self, say so. If not, push back upon the shelf of silence all your thoughts, till faith shall come... —*Ella Wheeler Wilcox*

Faith moves mountains, but you have to keep pushing while you are praying... —*Mason Cooley*

Faith is believing where we cannot prove...
—*Alfred L. Tennyson*

Faith is not a thing which one "loses," we merely cease to shape our lives by it... —*George Bernaos*

Faith is devotion to God... —*Jacob Katz*

Faith is the capacity of the soul to perceive the abiding...in the transitory, the invisible in the visible... —*Leon Baeck*

Faith is like a fond mother who can never fail to save her trusting son from dangerous situations... —*Tripura Rahasya*

There is a thing the world calls disappointment but there is no such word in the dictionary of faith... —*John Newton*

Only the person who has faith in himself is able to be faithful to others... —*Erich Fromm*

Faith is an invisible and invincible magnet, and attracts to itself whatever it fervently desires and calmly and persistently expects ... —*Ralph W. Trine*

Faith is the flame that lights the candle of life and without it we are fallow... —*William R. Miller*

Ultimately faith is the only key to the universe. The final meaning of human existence, and the answers to the questions on which all our happiness depends cannot be found in any other way... —*Thomas Merton*

Faith is affirming success before it comes. Faith is making claims to victory before it is achieved... —*Robert Schuller*

The reason why birds can fly and we can't is simply that they have perfect faith, for to have faith is to have wings... —*James M. Barrie*

Faith is the pencil of the soul that pictures heavenly things... —*Thomas Burbridge*

Reason is our soul's left hand, Faith her right; by these we reach divinity... —*John Donne*

A little faith brings your soul to heaven, but a lot of faith will bring heaven to your soul... —*Dwight L. Moody*

Our only protection against fear is faith... —*Ryllis G. Lynip*

Faith and Truth is the same thing—God's side is truth, our side is faith... —*Bernadette Roberts*

Falsehood

Lying to ourselves is more deeply ingrained than lying to others... —*Fyodor Dostoyevsky*

If there were no falsehood in the world, there would be no

doubt; if there were no doubt, there would be no inquiry; if no inquiry, no wisdom... —*Walter S. Landor*

Man cannot play false to his heredity forever. Spawned by the gods, he must return to them... —*Paul Brunton*

Falsehood, like poison, will generally be rejected when administered alone, but when blended with wholesome ingredients, may be swallowed unperceived...

—*Richard Whatley*

Falsehood often lurks upon the tongue of him, who, by self praise, seeks to enhance his value in the eyes of others...

—*James G. Bennett*

Falsehoods not only disagree with truths, but usually quarrel among themselves... —*Daniel Webster*

Falsehood may have its hour, but it has no future...

—*Francois D. Pressense*

The most dangerous of all follies is perverted wisdom...

—*Eliphas Levi*

Fame

Fame is a fickle food upon a shifting plate...

—*Emily Dickinson*

Man in blessing others finds his highest fame...

—*Sara J. Hale*

One of the drawbacks of Fame is that one can never escape from it... —*Nellie Melba*

Those who make fame and the opinion of others their life's goal are always panting after it like a thirsty dog. They never find peace... —*Martin Grey*

Fame is sometimes like unto a kind of mushroom, which Pliny recounts to be the greatest miracle in nature because growing and having no root... —*Thomas Fuller*

Good fame is like a fire; when you have kindled it, you may easily preserve it; but if you extinguish it, you will not easily kindle it again... —*Francis Bacon*

Love of fame is the last thing even the wise give up... —*Tacitus*

Let us satisfy our own consciences, and trouble not ourselves by looking for fame...If we deserve it, we shall attain it; if we deserve it not, we cannot force it... —*Seneca*

Fame is an empty bubble... —*James Grainger*

Fame to the ambitious, is like saltwater to the thirsty—the more one gets, the more one wants... —*Emil Ebers*

What is fame? A many colored cloak, without warmth, without protection... —*Berthold Auerbach*

Fame is like a river, that beareth up things light and swollen, and drowns things weighty and solid... —*Francis Bacon*

Worldly fame is but a breath of wind that blows now this way, and now that, and changes name as it changes direction... —*Dante Alighieri*

He who seeks to gain fame and reputation shall lose it; he who does not seek fame and reputation shall gain it... —*The Talmud*

Fate/Destiny

If you would know the meaning of destiny, understand that it is not a map of where you are going to go. Rather, it is where you will go if you will flow with existence without a struggle... —*Ormand McGill*

Chance is the pseudonym of God when he did not want to sign... —*Anatole France*

Fate! There is no fate. Between the thought and the success God is the only agent...Fate is not the ruler, but the servant of Providence... —*Edward Bulwer–Lytton*

Destiny is not a matter of chance; it is a matter of choice. It is not a thing to be waited for; it is a thing to be achieved... —*William J. Bryan*

Nothing comes by chance, for in all the world there is no such thing as chance... —*Ralph W. Trine*

Whatever limits us we call Fate... —*Ralph W. Emerson*

Men at sometime are masters of their fate. The fault...is not in the stars, but in ourselves...that we are underlings... —*William Shakespeare*

Chance is a word void of sense; nothing can exist without a cause... —*Voltaire*

Chance is the nickname for Providence... —*Nicolas Chamfort*

The harder you work, the luckier you get... —*Gary Player*

Fate is the friend of the good, the guide of the wise, the tyrant of the foolish, the enemy of the bad... —*William R. Alger*

Fault finding

Criticism is futile because it puts a man on the defensive, and usually makes a man strive to justify himself... —*Dale Carnegie*

Everybody is unique. Compare not yourself with anybody else lest you spoil God's curriculum... —*Baal Shem Tov*

Whoever is aware of his own failings will not find fault with the failings of other men... —*James Ross*

The girl who cannot dance says the band can't play... —*Yiddish proverb*

You have in yourself all the faults which you scorn in others... —*Will Durant*

The faultfinder will find faults even in Paradise...
—*Henry D. Thoreau*

Never throw mud. You may miss your mark. And you will certainly have dirty hands... —*Joseph Parker*

Faults of the head are punished in this world, those of the heart in another... —*Charles C. Colton*

See everything: overlook a good deal; correct a little...
—*Pope John XXIII*

If you are pleased at finding faults, you are displeased at finding perfections... —*John K. Lavater*

And why do you behold the mote that is in your brother's eye, and do not consider the beam in your own eye...
—*Jesus*

Faults are thick where love is thin... —*James Howell*

You will find it less easy to uproot faults than to choke them by gaining virtue... —*John Ruskin*

Anyone can blame; it takes a specialist to praise...
—*Konstantin Stanislavsky*

How much easier it is to be critical than to be correct...
—*Benjamin Disraeli*

Stop complaining about the management of the universe. Look around for a place to sow a few seeds of happiness...
—*Henry Van Dyke*

We should correct our own faults by seeing how uncomely they appear in others... —*Francis Beaumont*

Every one is eagle - eyed to see another's faults and deformity... —*John Dryden*

Quarrels would not last long if the fault were only on one side... —*Francois La Rochefoucauld*

When we condemn other people, we generally indirectly mean to flatter ourselves... —*John S. Blackie*

The world is full of wooden people who are always doing their best to whittle others down... —*Puzant K. Thomajan*

Another's "fault" is certainly a most valuable gift to me. It is a mirror which allows me to choose another reflection... —*Hugh Prather*

Love sees no faults... —*Thomas Fuller*

Finding fault with others, developing skill at discovering weakness and inconsistency in others, will begin to eat into your peace of mind. If you keep it up forever, it will eventually rob you of all the joys of life... —*James Mangan*

Do you never look at yourself when you criticize another person?... —*Plautus*

It is only imperfection that complains of what is imperfect. The more perfect we are, the more gentle and quiet we become towards the defects of others... —*Francois Fenelon*

Always remember that a person that you find fault with a great deal, will finally rebel... —*E.W. Howe*

Everything that irritates us about others can lead us to an understanding of ourselves... —*Carl Jung*

Fear

Never fear uncertainty. There is never anything to fear in uncertainty. Fear arises because men want to be certain according to their terms, but these terms are all wrong. It is quite possible to have a thousand uncertainties and not have a single fear... —*Vernon Howard*

We promise according to our hopes and perform according to our fears... —*Francois La Rochefoucauld*

No passion so effectively robs the mind of all its powers of acting and reasoning as fear... —*Edmund Burke*

Fear is only an illusion. It is the illusion that creates the feeling of separateness—the false sense of isolation that exists only in your imagination... —*Jeraldine Sanders*

Do the thing you fear and the death of fear is certain... —*Ralph W. Emerson*

Fear is not created by the world around us, but in the mind... —*Elizabeth Gawain*

Happy is the man who has trampled underfoot his fears and can laugh at the approach of all-subduing death... —*Virgil*

The best way to confront your fears is to stop avoiding the situation you're most afraid of... —*David D. Burns*

There are two kinds of people: those who are paralyzed by fear, and those who are afraid but go ahead anyway... —*Brooke Knapp*

Fear is more disgraceful than failure... —*Robert Schuller*

Fears are caused by a misuse of imagination... —*Herbert Casson*

Fear makes the wolf bigger than he is... —*German proverb*

Fear is the sand in the machinery of life... —*E. Stanley Jones*

Faith in yourself and faith in God are the key to the mastery of fear... —*Harold Sherman*

Let nothing disturb you. Let nothing frighten you. Everything passes away except God... —*Teresa of Avila*

The most dramatic and usually the most effective remedy for fear is direct action... —*William Burnham*

Fear makes strangers of people who should be friends...
—*Shirley MacLaine*

Fear and love can never be experienced at the same time. It is always our choice as to which of these emotions we want...
—*Gerald Jampolsky*

Worry is a form of fear, and all forms of fear produce fatigue. A man who has learned not to fear will find the fatigue of daily life enormously diminished...
—*Bertrand Russell*

All my fears and cares are of this world; if there is another, an honest man has nothing to fear from it... —*Robert Burns*

Forgiveness

An apology is the superglue of life. It can repair just about everything... —*Lynn Johnston*

How unhappy is he who cannot forgive himself...
—*Publilius Syrus*

When a deep injury is done us, we can never recover until we forgive... —*Alan Paton*

We cannot love unless we have accepted forgiveness, and the deeper our experience of forgiveness is, the greater is our love... —*Paul Tillich*

When Christ says,"Forgive your enemies," it is not for the sake of the enemy, but for one's own sake that he says so...
—*Oscar Wilde*

Love is an act of endless forgiveness... —*Peter Ustinov*

When you go to bed at night, have for your pillow three things—love, hope and forgiveness. And you will awaken in the morning with a song in your heart... —*Victor Hugo*

If you haven't forgiven yourself something, how can you forgive others?... —*Dolores Huerta*

Without forgiveness life is governed by...an endless cycle of resentment and retaliation... —*Robert Assagioli*

It is easier to forgive an enemy than to forgive a friend... —*William Blake*

Forgiveness is another word for letting go... —*Matthew Fox*

It is more noble to forgive than to revenge an injury... —*Benjamin Franklin*

He who forgives, ends the quarrel... —*African proverb*

In this life, if you have anything to pardon, pardon quickly. Slow forgiveness is little better than no forgiveness... —*Arthur W. Pinero*

If you forgive others their failings, your heavenly Father will forgive yours; but if you do not forgive others, your Father will not forgive your failings either... —*Jesus*

To understand everything means to forgive everything... —*French proverb*

Here is the mental treatment guaranteed to cure every ill that flesh is heir to: sit for half an hour every night and mentally forgive everyone against whom you have any ill will or antipathy... —*Charles Fillmore*

In heaven the only art of living is forgetting and forgiving... —*William Blake*

On the wings of forgiveness is carried all other wisdom... —*Honey J. Rubin*

Freedom

You cannot parcel out freedom in pieces because freedom is all or nothing... —*Tertullian*

Freedom is a new religion... —*Heinrich Heine*

Men are freest when they are most unconscious of freedom...
—David H. Lawrence

No one is free who is a slave to the flesh... *—Seneca*

Freedom is just another word for nothing left to lose...
—Janis Joplin

Our freedom can be measured by the amount of things we can walk away from... *—Vernon Howard*

There can be no freedom without the freedom to fail...
—Eric Hoffer

Those who deny freedom to others deserve it not for themselves... *—Abraham Lincoln*

The price of freedom is responsibility, but it is a bargain, because freedom is priceless... *—Hugh Downs*

You are your own jailer... *—Farid Attar*

No man is free who cannot command himself; liberty exists in proportion to wholesome restraint... *—Daniel Webster*

Freedom is not truly freedom while constraint can still limit it... *—Karlfried G. Durckheim*

Freedom is nothing but a chance to be better...
—Albert Camus

The more I understand about myself, the more I understand about the world. The more I understand about my world, the freer I am from it... *—Donald Curtis*

The freer you feel yourself in the presence of another, the more free he is... *—John K. Lavater*

Your freedom to choose a positive attitude is the treasure God will let no one take from you... *—Robert Schuller*

Freedom is the power to create out of nothing, the power of the spirit to create out of itself... *—Nikolay Berdyayev*

Man is free at the moment he wishes to be... —*Voltaire*

The path of freedom is blocked much more by those who wish to obey than by those who wish to command...
—*M.D. Petre*

Liberty is the one thing you can't have unless you give it to others... —*William A. White*

Freedom is what you do with what's been done to you...
—*Jean–Paul Sartre*

Freedom is the right to choose: the right to create for yourself the alternatives of choice. Without the possibility of choice and the exercise of choice, a man is not a man but a member, an instrument, a thing... —*Archibald MacLeish*

Freedom will cost you the mask you have on, the mask that feels so comfortable and is so hard to shed off, not because it fits so well but because you have been wearing it so long...
—*Florinda Donner*

Friendship

Be a friend to thyself, and others will be so too...
—*Thomas Fuller*

Real friendship is exchanging secrets, rolling over like a puppy and exposing the soft underbelly... —*Adair Lara*

We can be our own best friend or we can be our own worst enemies... —*Ralph W. Trine*

Two may talk together under the same roof for many years, yet never really meet; and two others at first speech are old friends... —*Mary Catherwood*

Old friends are best. King James used to call for his old shoes; they were easiest on his feet... —*John Selden*

A friend is a person with whom you dare to be yourself...
—*Frank Crane*

A real friend is one who walks in when the rest of the world walks out... —*Walter Winchell*

False friends are like a shadow, keeping close to us while we walk in the sunshine, but leaving us the instant we cross into the shade... —*Christian Bovee*

Friendship is so much more than a word, a handshake, and a smile. It's the ability to see the inner beauty in someone... —*Vonda K. Van Dyke*

Genius

An expert is one who does not have to think. He knows... —*Frank L. Wright*

There is no great genius without some touch of madness... —*Seneca*

Genius is only the power of making continuous efforts... —*Elbert Hubbard*

Genius springs from the soul that dares to drink at the fountains of inspiration in the garden of God...—*Fenwick Holmes*

Genius...means little more than the faculty of perceiving in an unhabitual way... —*William James*

The great secret of genius is to carry the spirit of the child into old age... —*Thomas Huxley*

Genius finds its own road, and carries its own lamp... —*Robert A. Willmott*

Everyone is born a genius, but the process of living de–geniuses them... —*Buckminster Fuller*

Genius is only a superior power of seeing... —*John Ruskin*

Genius must be born; it can never be taught... —*John Dryden*

Genius does what it must, and talent does what it can...
—*Edward Bulwer-Lytton*

Genius on earth is God giving Himself. Whenever a masterpiece appears, a distribution of God is taking place...
—*Victor Hugo*

The highest genius is willingness and ability to do hard work...
—*Robert S. MacArthur*

Common sense is genius in homespun...
—*Alfred N. Whitehead*

A genius is one who stands at both ends of a perspective...
—*Elbert Hubbard*

Genius is the energy which collects, combines, amplifies, and animates... —*Samuel Johnson*

With the stone we cast at them, geniuses build new roads for us... —*Paul Eldridge*

Constant effort and frequent mistakes are the stepping-stones of genius... —*Elbert Hubbard*

The essence of genius is to know what to overlook...
—*William James*

What is called genius is the abundance of life or health...
—*Henry D. Thoreau*

Genius is one percent inspiration and ninety nine percent perspiration... —*Thomas Edison*

Giving

Generosity lies less in giving much than in giving at the right moment... —*Jean La Bruyere*

It is one of the beautiful compensations of this life that no one can sincerely try to help another without helping himself... —*Charles D. Warner*

There is no happiness in having or in getting, but only in giving... —*Henry Drummond*

Supply is not getting; supply is giving. The bread that you cast upon the water is the bread that comes back to you... —*Joel Goldsmith*

Your giving is sacred and therefore should be kept secret. It is wise to give quietly with no strings attached... —*Catherine Ponder*

Give, and it shall be given unto you, good measure, pressed down...and running over...For with the same measure you give to others it shall be measured to you again... —*Jesus*

Money giving is a very good criterion of a person's mental health. Generous people are rarely mentally ill people... —*Karl Menninger*

Generosity gives help rather than advice... —*Luc de Clapiers Vauvenargues*

Unhappiness is the hunger to get; happiness is the hunger to give... —*William G. Jordan*

We can only give what we have in our purse... —*Henri F. Amiel*

Most of the joy of living comes out of true giving—giving without strings attached... —*Gary Emery*

The real test of a man is not: How much has he got? The measure of a man is: How much does he give that he can afford to give... —*Fred Van Amburgh*

The giver is greater than the gift... —*Eknath Easwaran*

Our true acquisitions lie only in our charities; we gain only as we give... —*William Simms*

Fill yourselves first and then only will you be able to give to others... —*Augustine*

It is more blessed to give than to receive... —*Paul of Tarsus*

God has the power to give and to take away; but if anything is taken away it is only to make room for something far better... —*Henry T. Hamblin*

In the sphere of material things, giving means being rich. Not he who has much is rich, but he who gives much... —*Erich Fromm*

In this world it is not what we take up, but what we give up, that makes us rich... —*Henry W. Beecher*

He who gives freely is apt to grow richer in heart, though he grows poorer in purse... —*George H. Hepworth*

You can't live a perfect day without doing something for someone who will never be able to repay you... —*John Wooden*

A bit of fragrance always clings to the hand that gives you roses... —*Chinese proverb*

They who scatter with one hand, gather with two, not always in coin, but in kind. Nothing multiplies so much as kindness... —*John Wray*

He that gives all, though but little, gives much, because God looks not at the quantity of the gift, but to the quality of the givers... —*Francis Quarles*

Do not limit what you give, limit what you take... —*Napoleon Hill*

Giving is most blessed and most acceptable when the donor remains completely anonymous... —*Maimonides*

To receive everything, one must open one's hands and give... —*Taisen Deshimaru*

Goals

You can't get anywhere unless you know where to start from and where to go... —*Lionel Barrymore*

If you don't know where you are going, you will probably wind up somewhere else... —*Laurence J. Peter*

Know what you want to do—then do it. Make straight for your goal and go undefeated in spirit to the end... —*Ernestine Schumann–Heink*

Goals are simply tools to focus your energy in positive directions, they can be changed as your priorities change, new ones added, and others dropped... —*O. Carl Simonton*

If you have no goals, your thoughts will take you toward what you think about most... —*Andrew Matthews*

The reason most people never reach their goals is that they don't define them, or ever seriously consider them as believable or achievable... —*Denis Waitley*

It must be borne in mind that the tragedy of life does not lie in not reaching your goals, the tragedy lies in not having any goals to reach... —*Benjamin I. Mays*

Goals are absolutely essential, for goals give meaning to life... —*Victor Frankl*

Seeking means to have a goal; but finding means to be free, to be receptive, to have no goal... —*Hermann Hesse*

God

Once you've seen the face of God, you see the same face on everyone you meet... —*Deng Ming–Dao*

The helping of man by man is God... —*Ancient Greek saying*

The eye with which I see God is the same eye by which God sees me... —*Meister Eckhart*

Everywhere you look in science, it becomes the harder to understand the universe without God... —*Robert Herrman*

I cannot imagine a God who rewards and punishes the objects of His creation, whose purposes are modeled after our own—a God, in short, who is a reflection of human frailty...
—*Albert Einstein*

God is no fairy story, no wishful thinking, no joke, no ancient legend...God is real. God is... —*P.M.H. Atwater*

Do you need proof of God? Does one light a torch to see the sun?... —*Chinese proverb*

I could not say I believe. I know! I have had the experience of being gripped by something that is stronger than myself, something that people call God... —*Carl Jung*

The most basic thing you can say about God is that God is love... —*C. Alan Anderson*

God is an experience, and no one knows God until he has had that experience... —*Joel Goldsmith*

We can know what God is not, but we cannot know what He is... —*Augustine*

God is a light that is never darkened... —*Francis Quarles*

We are, in the hands of God, like blocks of marble in the hands of sculptors... —*Alphonsus Liguori*

God is day–night, winter–summer, love–hate, war–peace, abundance–want, heat–cold, death–life, youth–age, waking—asleep, creation—destruction... —*Heraclitus*

When people are loving, brave, truthful, charitable, God is present... —*Harold Kushner*

The ancient hieroglyphic for God was the figure of an eye upon a sceptre, to denote that he sees and rules all things...
—*John M. Barker*

Belief in God is acceptance of the basic principle that the universe makes sense, that there is behind it an ultimate purpose... —*Carl W. Miller*

God is that which has no definition... —*Joseph Albo*

I had a thousand questions to ask God; but when I met Him they all fled and didn't seem to matter...
—*Christopher Morley*

Man without God is a bubble in the sea, a single grain of sand on an infinite beach... —*Pincus Goodblatt*

God created man in His Image and likeness, and then man returned the compliment and created God in his own image and likeness... —*Jean J. Rousseau*

The deepest need of men is not food and clothing and shelter, important as they are. It is God... —*Thomas R. Kelly*

On the day I first really believed in God, for the first time life made sense to me and the world had meaning...
—*Dag Hammarskjöld*

God is a blank sheet upon which nothing is found but what you yourself have written... —*Martin Luther*

God outside us is an hypothesis; God inside us is an experience... —*Harry E. Fosdick*

God is a fountain flowing into itself... —*St. Dionysius*

God is the sum of all possibilities... —*Isaac Bashevis Singer*

The things which are impossible with men are possible with God... —*Jesus*

God does not dwell in a body, so we cannot define Him in a material way. God is a spirit... —*Billy Graham*

When man shall see God, he shall see himself and not until then... —*Frater Achad*

Wherever there are no limits, where Infinity and Eternity and Immortality exist, that is where God is...

—*Omraam M. Aivanhov*

God's Will

There is nothing great, there is nothing holy, there is nothing wise, there is nothing fair, but to depend wholly upon God, like a child does and can do only what is bidden...

—*Jeanne–Marie Guyon*

Life has taught me that it knows better plans than we can imagine, so I try to submerge my own desires...into a calm willingness to accept what comes... —*Julia Seton*

We must follow, not force providence...

—*William Shakespeare*

Learn to will what God wishes, and everything you want will certainly happen... —*Eliphas Levi*

God is our owner, we are His property; His providence works for our good... —*Immanuel Kant*

Those people who are not governed by God will be ruled by tyrants... —*William Penn*

God gives the perfect blueprint for each upcoming experience and we either wisely go along with God's plan or we foolishly refuse to follow His lead... —*C. Alan Anderson*

Desire and pray always that God's will be perfectly fulfilled in you... —*Thomas à Kempis*

Remember that you are an actor in a play, and of such sort as the Author chooses, whether long or short. If it be His good pleasure to assign you the part of a beggar, a ruler, or a simple citizen, it is yours to play the role fitly. For your business is to act well the part assigned you; to choose it, is Another's... —*Epictetus*

It is not within the law of God that man should live in poverty, destitute. It is God's will that man should have plenty, heaped up, pressed together and running over...

—*Frater Achad*

If we make God's will our law, then God's promise shall be our support and comfort, and we shall find every burden light, and every duty a joy... —*Tryon Edwards*

To a good man to serve the will of God, it is in the truest and best sense to serve himself... —*John Smith, the Platonist*

No servant of God can be more than a channel or instrument. God works through His servants. They do not work for God, but God through them. God raises up His own instruments, guides them, trains them, and, if found worthy, uses them... —*Henry T. Hamblin*

The highest peace which the soul can enjoy is to know itself as much as possible united with God's will... —*Angelus Silesius*

The study of God's word, for the purpose of discovering God's will, is a secret discipline which has formed the greatest characters... —*James W. Alexander*

God is the master of scenes; we must not choose which part we shall act; it concerns us only to be careful that we do it well... —*Jeremy Taylor*

It is not everyone who says to me "Lord! Lord!" who will get into the Kingdom of Heaven, but only those who do the will of my Father... —*Jesus*

The superior man lives quietly and calmly, waiting for the will of Heaven, while the average man does what is full of risk, looking out for turns of luck... —*Confucius*

There is not in the world a kind of life more sweet and delightful than that of a continual walk with God. Those only can comprehend it who practice and experience it...

—*Brother Lawrence*

The surest method of arriving at a knowledge of God's eternal purpose about us is to be found in the right use of the present moment... —*Frederick W. Faber*

Golden Rule

"Do not do to others what you would not have them do to you" is one of the most fundamental principles of ethics. But it is equally justifiable to state: Whatever you do to others, you also do to yourself... —*Eric Fromm*

Treat your inferiors as you would be treated by your betters... —*Seneca*

In everything do to others as you would have them do to you, for this is the law of the prophets... —*Jesus*

Pity the misfortunes of others; rejoice in the well being of others; help those who are in want; save men in danger; rejoice at the success of others; and sympathize with their reverses, even as though you were in their place...
—*Tai–Shang*

Regard your neighbor's gain as your own gain, and our neighbor's loss as your own loss...
—*T'ai Shang Kan Ying P'ien*

Behave to your servants as you desire God to behave to you...
—*Philo*

Our conscience teaches us it is right, our reason teaches us it is useful, that men should live according to the Golden Rule... —*W. Winwood Reade*

Good

The Infinite Goodness has such wide arms that it takes whatever turns to it... —*Dante Alighieri*

Our original nature is purely good. It is not possible to add anything to this original state... —*Wang Ying Ming*

Goodness is the only investment that never fails...
—Henry D. Thoreau

By the presence of good, evil is cast out, just as by the presence of light, the darkness disappears... *—Ernest Holmes*

Doing good to others is not a duty. It is a joy, for it increases your own health and happiness... *—Zoroaster*

All good things which exist are the fruits of originality...
—John S. Mill

The work an unknown good man has done is like a vein of water flowing hidden underground, secretly making the ground green... *—Thomas Carlyle*

Wise men appreciate all men, for they see the good in each and know how hard it is to make anything good...
—Baltazar Gracian

The power generated of ten minds for good is superior to that of ten thousand minds acting on a lower motive. But it is a silent power. It moves in mysterious ways. It is noiseless. It makes no show of open opposition. It uses no methods of effort through tongue or arm or physical force...
—Prentice Mulford

Do not waste yourself in rejections nor bark against the bad, but chant the beauty of the good... *—Ralph W. Emerson*

Good people are good because they've come to the wisdom through failure... *—William Saroyan*

Waste no time arguing what a good man should be. Be one...
—Marcus Aurelius

Goodness is easier to recognize than to define...
—W.H. Auden

The tendency of man's nature to good is like the tendency of water to flow downwards... *—Menicus*

Grace

Grace is something you can never get but only be given...
—*Frederick Buechner*

Do not fall into the trap of trying to force some results. Don't forget we do not deserve anything. Everything is a gift—spontaneous or not at all... —*Lucy Cornellssen*

Grace is a certain beauty of the soul, which wins the divine love... —*Thomas Aquinas*

We must empty ourselves if we are to be filled. When the mind has poured out all its thoughts, a vacuum is created. But this can only last for a few seconds. Then a mysterious influx of divine life will enter... —*Paul Brunton*

The little word "grace" is like a small window that opens out on to a great landscape... —*Alexander Maclaren*

The sure sign of grace is...the desire to go against all selfish desires... —*Eknath Easwaran*

Grace comes into the soul, as the morning sun into the world: first a dawning, then a light, and at last the sun in his full and excellent brightness... —*Thomas Adams*

Grace is the mastery of truth, the teacher of discipline, the light of the heart, the comforter of affliction, the banisher of sorrow, the nurse of devotion... —*Thomas à Kempis*

Grace binds you with far stronger cords than the cords of duty or obligation can bind you. Grace is free, but when once you take it you are bound forever to the Giver...
—*E. Stanley Jones*

The growth of grace is like the polishing of metals. There is first an opaque surface; and by and by, you see a spark darting out, then a strong light; till at length it sends back a perfect image of the sun that shines upon it...
—*Edward Payson*

Gratitude

Don't drown the man who taught you to swim...Do not kick down the ladder by which you climbed... —*C.H. Spurgeon*

Gratitude is the bottom line of happiness...
—*Lewis B. Smedes*

The more we thank God for the blessings we receive, the more we open the way for further blessings...
—*Betty J. Eadie*

If you can't have what you want, be grateful for what you have. Keep thinking constantly of all the big things you have to be thankful for instead of complaining about the little things that annoy you... —*Dale Carnegie*

To stand on one leg and prove the existence of God is a very different thing from going down on one's knees and thanking Him... —*Sören Kierkegaard*

A thankful heart is not only the greatest virtue, but the parent of all other virtues... —*Cicero*

If anyone could tell you the shortest, surest way to all happiness and perfection, he must tell you to make a rule to yourself to thank and praise God for everything that happens to you. For it is certain that whatever calamity happens to you, if you thank and praise God for it, you turn it into a blessing... —*William Law*

God has no need for our worship. It is we who need to show our gratitude for what we have received...
—*Thomas Aquinas*

None is more impoverished than the one who has no gratitude...Gratitude is a currency that we can mint for ourselves, and spend without fear of bankruptcy...
—*Fred Van Amburgh*

Gratitude is a vaccine, an antitoxin, and an antiseptic...
—*John H. Jowett*

If the only prayer you say in your entire life is "Thank you," that will suffice... *—Meister Eckhart*

The people who are successful are those who are grateful for everything they have...Giving thanks for what we have, always opens the door for more to come, and ungratefulness always closes the door... *—Alan Cohen*

It is impossible to be negative while we are giving thanks... *—Donald Curtis*

Gratitude to God should be habitual... *—Charles Simmons*

The worship most acceptable to God comes from a thankful and cheerful heart... *—Plutarch*

Greatness

We are very near to greatness: one step and we are safe: can we not take the leap?... *—Ralph W. Emerson*

Our greatest weaknesses are always the flip side of our greatest strengths... *—Judith Sills*

The first element of greatness is fundamental humbleness... *—Margot Asquith*

There can be no greatness in things. Things cannot be great. The only greatness is unselfish love... *—Henry Drummond*

There never was yet a truly great man that was not at the same time truly virtuous... *—Benjamin Franklin*

The great man always thinks of virtue; the common man thinks of comfort... *—Confucius*

A great man is one who can have power and not abuse it... *—Henry L. Doherty*

It is the test of greatness in a man that he should be able to see greatness in others, and give them ungrudging credit for it... *—John Ruskin*

Everything great is not always good, but all good things are great... —*Demosthenes*

The great men of the earth are but marking stones on the road of humanity... —*Giuseppe Mazzini*

He is the great man who uses earthenware dishes as if they were silver; and he is equally great who uses silver as if it were earthenware... —*Seneca*

Some are born great; some achieve greatness; and some have greatness thrust upon them... —*William Shakespeare*

The greatest...is to bear defeat without losing heart... —*Robert Ingersoll*

A great man never loses the simplicity of a child.... —*Confucius*

Grief

The true way to mourn the dead is to take care of the living who belong to them... —*Edmund Burke*

If you harbor grief, and give your sorrows vent, they will grow greater every day. They will absorb your very life until at last you will be naught but grief, wet down with bitter tears... —*The Aquarian Gospel*

Grief drives men into habits of serious reflection, sharpens the understanding and softens the heart... —*John Adams*

Grieve not; though the journey of life be bitter, and the end unseen, there is no road which does not lead to an end... —*Haftz*

Grief is a wound that needs attention in order to heal... —*Judy Tatelbaum*

Let us not lament too much the passing of our friends. They are not dead but simply gone before us along the road which all must travel... —*Antiphanes*

He who is dead and gone, honor with remembrance, not with tears... —*John Chrysostom*

Do not mourn over dying things: look to the east, give your heart to the future. The trees have fallen, but the shoots remain. Reach out your arms to bless those yet to be born... —*Victor de Laprade*

Grief is selfish. It is indulged in for self gratification, not for love. Cosmic man knows the beauty and unreality of death... —*Walter Russell*

The loss of friends by the transition we call death will not cause sorrow to the soul that has come into the higher realization, for he knows there is no such thing as death, for each of us is not only a partaker, but an eternal partaker, of this Infinite Life... —*Ralph W. Trine*

The first and necessary step of grief is discovering what you have lost. The next step is discovering what is left, what is possible... —*John Schneider*

Every substantial grief has twenty shadows, and most of them shadows of your own making... —*Sydney Smith*

Sorrow's best antidote is employment... —*Edward Young*

There is no greater grief than to remember days of joy when misery is at hand... —*Dante Alighieri*

Grief is itself a medicine... —*William Cowper*

Grief is a tree that tears for its fruit... —*Philemon*

Nothing becomes offensive so quickly as grief. When fresh, it finds someone to console it, but when it becomes chronic, it is ridiculed, and rightly... —*Seneca*

Growth

The human way of growing is unique; it has no rules, and can occur in many ways... —*Marsha Sinetar*

We cannot stand still. We must grow. We must keep on improving ourself. This is life's main issue. All the experiences of life are for the purpose of making us more wonderful...
—Elinor MacDonald

Pain is the price we pay for growing... *—Alice H. Rice*

Nothing grows well in the shade of a big tree...
—Constantin Brancusi

We grow by leaving behind our comfortable old beliefs...
—Meredith Young–Sowers

The moment a man begins to think for himself, that moment he begins to grow... *—Fred Van Amburgh*

You will not grow if you sit in a beautiful flower garden, but you will grow if you are sick, if you are in pain, if you experience losses, and if you do not put your head in the sand, but take the pain and learn to accept it, not as a curse or punishment, but as a gift to you with a very, very specific purpose... *—Elisabeth Kubler–Ross*

All growth...is the result of risk taking... *—Jude Wanniski*

The two great laws of life are growth and decay. When things stop growing they begin to die. This is true of men, business or nations... *—Charles R. Gow*

When you see the value of contiued growth, the circumstances around you become stepping stones...
—Clyde M. Narrimore

I am still learning... *—Michelangelo's motto*

Progress and growth are impossible if you always do things the way you've always done things... *—Wayne Dyer*

Habits

Your habits can be your friends or your enemies; they can help you or hurt you... *—Maxwell Maltz*

Habits change into character... —*Ovid*

Have you ever fully realized that life is, after all, merely a series of habits, and that it lies entirely within one's own power to determine just what that series shall be?...

—*Ralph W. Trine*

Tension is a habit. Relaxing is a habit. And bad habits can be broken, good habits formed... —*Dale Carnegie*

We are what we repeatedly do. Excellence then, is not an act, but a habit... —*Aristotle*

Habits are like a cable. We weave a strand of it every day and soon it cannot be broken... —*Horace Mann*

Our habits, our addictions, our devotions, are either stepping stones or stumbling blocks... —*Fred Van Amburgh*

Men cling to the opinions of habits... —*Maimonides*

As a single footstep will not make a path on the earth, so a single thought will not make a pathway in the mind. To make a deep physical path, we walk again and again. To make a deep mental path, we must think over and over the kind of thoughts we wish to dominate our lives...

—*Henry D. Thoreau*

Habit becomes a sort of second nature, which supplies a motive for many actions...Great is the power of habit...

—*Cicero*

Whenever you are angry, be assured that it is not only a present habit, but that you have increased a habit, and added fuel. If you desire not to have an angry temper, then, do not feed the habit. Give it nothing to help its increase...

—*Epictetus*

Habit, if not resisted, soon becomes necessity...

—*Augustine*

The man who interferes with another's habits has the worst one... —*Henry S. Hawkins*

Habits are first cobwebs, then cables... —*Spanish proverb*

The absurd habit of trying to do many things at once is a great cause of confusion, frustration and nervousness... —*Maxwell Maltz*

The chains of habit are too weak to be felt until they are too strong to be broken... —*Samuel Johnson*

Habit is either the best of servants or the worst of masters... —*Nathaniel Emmons*

The daily habit of wishing everybody well, of feeling like wishing everybody God–speed, ennobles character, and beautifies and enriches life... —*Orison S. Marden*

Habit is the fly–wheel of civilization... —*Henry James*

Habit is habit, and not to be flung out the window by any man, but coaxed downstairs a step at a time... —*Mark Twain*

The mind is slow to unlearn what it has been long in learning... —*Seneca*

We first make our habits, and then our habits make us...All habits gather by unseen degress... —*John Dryden*

Any action repeated frequently will become habit, and it will remain habit until the mind is reprogrammed to eliminate the habit... —*Lois Wolfe–Morgan*

Good habits are so much easier to give up than bad habits... —*Somerset Maugham*

Happiness

If you ever find happiness by hunting for it, you will find it, as the old woman did her lost spectacles, safe on her nose all the time... —*Josh Billings*

A man is happy so long as he chooses to be happy and nothing can stop him... *Alexander Solzhenitsyn*

Happiness is a by–product of an effort to make someone else happy... *—Gretta B. Palmer*

If you want to be happy, be... *—Leo Tolstoy*

If one thinks one is happy, that is enough to be happy... *—Mme. de La Fayette*

We can never build happiness on the misery of other people.... *—Constance Warren*

The foolish man seeks happiness in the distance; the wise man grows it under his feet... *—James Oppenheim*

True happiness is to understand our duties toward God and man; to enjoy the present, without being anxious about the future; not to amuse ourselves with hopes and fears, but to rest satisfied with what we have... *—Seneca*

Happy is he who is good to others; miserable is he who expects good from others... *—Eknath Easwaran*

If your happiness depends on what somebody does...you do have a problem... *—Richard Bach*

Happiness is not a matter of events; it depends upon the tides of the mind... *—Alice Meynell*

Happiness is a butterfly, which, when pursued, is always just beyond your grasp, but which, if you will set down quietly, may alight upon you... *—Nathaniel Hawthorne*

Talk happiness. The world is sad enough without your woes. No path is wholly rough; look for the places that are smooth and clear... *—Ella Wheeler Wilcox*

Happiness is the greatest paradox in Nature. It can grow in any soil, live under any conditions. It defies environment. It comes from within... *—Norman V. Peale*

All men desire happiness. They do not know exactly what is meant by happiness, but they desire it just the same...
—James T. Mangan

Do not place your happiness in distant lands or in grandly imagined tasks; do well what you can do, until you can do greater things as well... *—Will Durant*

Remember that happiness is the way of travel—not a destination... *—Roy M. Goodman*

Happiness does not depend upon what we have, but it does depend on how we feel towards what we have...
—W.D. Hoard

Happiness is no other than soundness and perfection of the mind... *—Marcus Aurelius*

It is not easy to find happiness in ourselves, and it is not possible to find it elsewhere... *—Agnes Repplier*

Happiness depends upon what lies between the soles of the feet and the crown of your head... *—Honoré de Balzac*

Happiness comes not from without but from within. It comes not from the power of possession but from the power of appreciation... *—J. Walter Sylvester*

A great obstacle to happiness is to expect too much happiness... *—Bernard Fontanelle*

As long as we structure our lives in a way where our happiness is dependent upon something we cannot control, then we will experience pain... *—Anthony Robbins*

Happiness? It is an illusion to think that more comfort means more happiness. Happiness comes of the capacity to feel deeply, to enjoy simply, to think freely, to risk life, to be needed... *—Storm Jameson*

The happiness of your life depends upon the quality of your thoughts... *—Marcus Aurelius*

Happiness is a perfume you cannot pour on others without getting a few drops on yourself... —*Ralph W. Emerson*

Most people are about as happy as they make up their minds to be... —*Abraham Lincoln*

Man is meant for happiness, and this happiness is in him, in the satisfaction of the daily needs of his nature...
—*Leo Tolstoy*

Hatred

Hatred cannot last unless it is continuously nourished and stimulated... —*Edmund A. Brasset*

Hate traps us by binding us too tightly to our adversary...
—*Milan Kundera*

The one person perhaps in the world whom you most dislike is the very one to whom you are attaching yourself by a hook that is stronger than steel. Is this what you wish?...
—*Emmet Fox*

Hating people is like burning down your own house to get rid of a rat... —*Harry E. Fosdick*

Don't hate, it's too big a burden to bear...
—*Martin L. King, Sr.*

Men hate what they cannot understand... —*Moses Ibn Ezra*

We hate someone because we do not know them; and we will not know them because we hate them...
—*Charles C. Colton*

Hatred...is anger which has been allowed to dwell in the mind until it has hardened like so much cement...
—*Napoleon Hill*

Hate and fear breed a poison in the blood, which if continued, affects eyes, ears, nose and the organs of digestion. Therefore, it is not wise to hear and remember the unkind things others might say about you...'

—*Pythagoras*

He that hates his brother is in darkness, and walks in darkness, and knows not where he goes, because that darkness has blinded his eyes... —*Paul of Tarsus*

Health

The foundation of success in life is good health; that is the substratum of fortune; it is also the basis of happiness. A person cannot accumulate a fortune very well when he is sick. He has no ambition; no incentive; no force...

—*P.T. Barnum*

If you want to enjoy health, start this very moment to cleanse your consciousness of all wrong thinking and rid it of every thought except the thought of LOVE... —*James B. Schafer*

Poor health is not caused by something you don't have; it's caused by disturbing something that you already have. Healthy is not something that you need to get, it's something you have already if you don't disturb it...

—*Dean Ornish*

Extreme remedies are very appropriate for extreme diseases... —*Hippocrates*

Body and soul cannot be separated for purposes of treatment, for they are one and indivisible. Sick minds must be healed as well as sick bodies... —*C. Jeff Miller*

Man is ill because he is never still... —*Paracelsus*

Health is certainly more valuable than money because it is by health that money is procured... —*Samuel Johnson*

The greatest irritant to most people is not a lack of money or status, but ill health. Nothing shines brightly if we do not feel well... —*Margaret Stortz*

There is no curing a sick man who believes himself in health... —*Henri F. Amiel*

The secret of health is a pure heart and a well ordered mind... —*James Allen*

Fear kills more than disease... —*George Herbert*

Health is the groundwork for all happiness... —*Leigh Hunt*

Health enables us to serve purpose in our life, but it is not the purpose in life. One can serve purpose with impaired health... —*Rachel N. Remen*

All pleasures are tasteless without health. Sickness serves gruel... —*Fred Van Amburgh*

Cheerfulness is the principal ingredient in the composition of health... —*Arthur Murphy*

The greatest mistake a man can make is to sacrifice health for any other advantage... —*Arthur Schopenhauer*

Nature, time and patience are the three great physicians... —*Irish proverb*

Heart

The only thing that makes one place more attractive...than another is the quality of heart in it... —*Jane W. Carlyle*

The course of human history is determined, not by what happens in the skies, but by what takes place in the hearts of men... —*Arthur Keith*

A pure heart is the end of all religion and the beginning of divinity... —*James Allen*

The heart that breaks open can contain the whole universe... —*Joanna Macy*

It is only with the heart that one can see rightly; what is essential is invisible to the eye... —*Antoine de Saint-Exupery*

What comes from the heart, goes to the heart...
—Samuel T. Coleridge

The human heart...opens only to the heart that opens in return... *—Maria Edgeworth*

The heart sometimes finds out things that reason cannot...
—Robert Benson

Where your treasure is, there will your heart be also...
—Jesus

A kind heart is a fountain of gladness, making everything in its vicinity to freshen into smiles... *—Washington Irving*

Enter into your heart and labor in the presence of God who is always present there to help you. Fix your loving attention upon Him without any desire to feel or hear anything of God... *—John of the Cross*

When the heart is won, the understanding is easily convinced... *—Charles Simmons*

The heart of the fool is in his mouth, but the mouth of the wise man is in his heart... *—Benjamin Franklin*

When we know how to read our own hearts, we acquire wisdom of the hearts of others... *—Denis Diderot*

Find the god in your own heart and you will understand by direct intuition what all the great teachers, real mystics, true philosophers and inspired men have been trying to tell you by the tortuous method of using words... *—Paul Brunton*

Hearts are like flowers; they remain open to the softly falling dew, but shut up in the violent downpour of rain...
—Jean Paul Richter

Heaven & Hell

Heaven cannot be a place where we go when we die. If there were such a place, it wouldn't be heaven any longer after we got there...Heaven is a state of mind... —*Elinor MacDonald*

Heaven, the treasury of everlasting joy...
—*William Shakespeare*

The mind is its own place, and in itself can make a heaven of hell, and a hell of heaven... —*John Milton*

A guilty conscience is a hell on earth, and points to one beyond... —*Francis Beaumont*

The kingdom of heaven is not isolation of good from evil. It is the overcoming of good from evil... —*Alfred N. Whitehead*

We make our own heaven or our own hell, and the only heaven or hell that will ever be ours is that of our own making... —*Ralph W. Trine*

If men believe...that this present earth is the only heaven, they will strive all the more to make heaven of it...
—*Arthur Keith*

A good man is influenced by God himself, and has a kind of divinity within him; so it may be a question whether he goes to heaven, or heaven comes to him... —*Seneca*

Heaven is but the vision of fulfilled desire. And hell the shadow from a soul on fire... —*Omar Khayyam*

The only thing I could say for sure is that hell means separation from God... —*Billy Graham*

You have your paintbrush and colors. Paint paradise, and in you go... —*Nikos Kazantzakis*

Heaven is under our feet as well as over our heads...When you travel to the Celestial City, carry no letters of introduction—When you knock, ask to see God–none of the servants... —*Henry D. Thoreau*

Every person is the maker of his own heaven and hell...
—*Elinor MacDonald*

Here & Now

Not living in the present is a form of denial. It's easier to live in the past or future because then you don't have to be responsible for the present... —*Jane Hendrix*

Always hold fast to the present hour. Every state of duration, every second, is of infinite value... —*Johann W. Goethe*

The present time has one advantage over every other—it is our own... —*Charles C. Colton*

Every moment is a golden one for him who has the vision to recognize it as such... —*Henry Miller*

Doing the best at the moment puts you in the best place for the next moment... —*Oprah Winfrey*

One should learn from the past but one should not live in the past. My concern is to look to the future, learn from the past and deal with the present... —*George Fernandes*

Light tomorrow with today... —*Elizabeth B. Browning*

I've shut the door on yesterday and thrown the key away. Tomorrow holds no fear for me, since I have found today... —*Vivien Larrimore*

The art of enjoying every minute is to deal with only one minute at a time... —*Hilary Worth*

Nothing today need conform to anything of yesterday... —*Jesse Jennings*

The present is the necessary product of all the past, the necessary cause of all the future... —*Robert Ingersoll*

The time is now, the place is here. Stay in the present. You can do nothing to change the past, and the future will never come exactly as you plan or hope for... —*Dan Millman*

To live with God is to live always in the present, with him who is the eternal now... —*John A. T. Robinson*

Today is a new day. You will get out of it just what you put into it... —*Mary Pickford*

Yesterday is a cancelled check; tomorrow is a promissory note; today is the only cash you have—spend it wisely...
—*Kay Lyons*

Let each one examine his thoughts, and he will find them all occupied with the past and the future. We scarcely ever think of the present, and if we think of it, it is only to take light from it to arrange the future... —*Blaise Pascal*

Humility

Go and sit in the last place and then you will be invited to take the first... —*Jesus*

Never forget the hard times and the early days. Always remember where you came from... —*David Liederman*

The richest pearl in the...crown of graces is humility...
—*John M. Good*

If you are going to bow, bow low... —*Eastern proverb*

True humility is not an abject, groveling, self–despising spirit—it is but a right estimate of ourselves as God sees us...
—*Tryon Edwards*

God can do great things through the man who doesn't care who gets the credit... —*Robert Schuller*

No need to discount yourself in order to achieve humility; neither can you attain humility by overestimating what you are. Humility is your correct weight; no more, no less...
—*Fred Van Amburgh*

The way to make a good impression on other people is: Never "try" to make a good impression on them. Never act, or fail to act, purely for consciously contrived effect...
—*Maxwell Maltz*

Desire to sow no seed for your own harvesting; desire only to sow that seed the fruit of which will feed the world...
—*Mobel Collins*

The less a man thinks or knows about his virtues, the better we like him... —*Ralph W. Emerson*

If two angels were sent down from heaven—one to conduct an empire, and the other to sweep a street—they would feel no inclination to change employments...—*John Newton*

A man who really understands the strength of his position will never fail to be humble in his apology...
—*Margery Wilson*

Be willing to be a beginner every single morning...
—*Meister Eckhart*

Man is humble when the flaming fire of desires has become extinct... —*Al–Tirmidi*

When humility enters a man's soul, he is at last able to perceive that he does not live alone in the world but with millions of brothers, and that hidden in the heart of each is the same animating spirit... —*U.S. Anderson*

Discount the one who immediately starts out to tell you all about his accomplishments or achievements. If they are good and lasting, others will tell you about them...The big man does not have to brag. The little man thinks he must...
—*Fred Van Amburgh*

Of myself I can do nothing; the Father that dwells in me, He does the work... —*Jesus*

The gate of heaven...is so narrow that it admits only little ones... —*St. Bernard*

Nothing is in vain or without profit to the humble soul: like the bee, it takes its honey from the bitter herbs: it stands always in a state of divine growth, and everything that falls upon it is a dew of Heaven to it... —*William Law*

Humility is the most excellent cure for anger...

—*Jeremy Taylor*

As a dry stick is better disposed for burning than a wet stick, so a humble man is better disposed for faith than a know–it–all....

—*Fulton J. Sheen*

The humble soul is a temple of God, a seat of wisdom...

—*Johann Arndt*

It was pride that changed angels to devils; it is humility that makes men angels...

—*Augustine*

Even if you be otherwise perfect, you fail without humility...

—*The Talmud*

Hypocrisy

Let the world know you as you are, not as you think you should be, because sooner or later, if you think you are posing, you will forget the pose, and then where are you?...

—*Fannie Brice*

Hypocrisy is pretending to be perfect, and in the process, imposing a sense of judgement and guilt on those around you. Hypocrisy is giving everybody the verbal assurance that you are living up to your own standards, when you are really not...

—*Robert H. Schuller*

No man can, for any considerable time, wear one face to himself, and another to the multitude, without finally getting bewildered as to which is the true one...

—*Nathaniel Hawthorne*

One may smile and smile and be a villain still...

—*William Shakespeare*

I will have nothing to do with a man who can blow hot and cold with the same breath...

—*Aesop*

How can you say to another, "Let me take a speck out of

your eye!" Hypocrite! First remove the speck from your own eye, and then you will be able to remove that of your brother...
—*Jesus*

Actors are the only honest hypocrites. Their life is a voluntary dream; and the height of their ambition is to be beside themselves... —*William Hazlitt*

To thine own self be true, and it shall follow as night the day that thou cannot then be false to any man...
—*William Shakespeare*

Ignorance

When a stupid man is doing something he is ashamed of, he always declares that it is his duty... —*George B. Shaw*

People are never so near playing the fool as when they think themselves wise... —*Mary W. Montagu*

You are blind until your inner eyes of understanding are open... —*Archie Canfield*

The first reason for man's slavery is his ignorance, and above all, his ignorance of himself... —*George I. Gurdjieff*

Nothing in all the world is more dangerous than sincere ignorance and conscientious stupidity...
—*Martin Luther King, Jr.*

I have always observed that to succeed in the world one should seem like a fool, but be wise... —*Charles Montesquieu*

I have never met a man so ignorant that I couldn't learn something from him... —*Galileo Galilei*

A great deal of intelligence can be invested in ignorance when the need for illusion is deep... —*Saul Bellow*

The world is full of fools; and he who would not wish to see one, must not only shut himself up alone but must break his looking glass... —*Nicolas Boileau*

Fools with bookish knowledge are children with edged weapons; they hurt themselves, and put others in pain. The half learned is more dangerous than the simpleton...

—Johann G. Zimmerman

The recipe for perpetual ignorance is: be satisfied with your opinion and content with your knowledge...

—Elbert Hubbard

Impossible is a word only to be found in the dictionary of fools... *—Napoleon Bonaparte*

A fool can no more see his own folly than he can see his ears... *—William M. Thackeray*

A fool may be known by six things: anger, without cause; speech, without profit; change, without progress; inquiry, without object; putting trust in a stranger, and mistaking foes for friends... *—Arabian proverb*

Our lives are universally shortened by our ignorance...

—Herbert Spencer

It is better to be a beggar than ignorant... *—Aristippus*

To be overcome by pleasure is ignorance in the highest degree... *—Plato*

There are two kinds of fools: one says, 'This is old, therefore it is good'; the other says, 'This is new, therefore it is better'... *—William R. Inge*

If fifty million people say a foolish thing, it is still a foolish thing... *—Anatole France*

Let a fool hold his tongue and he will pass for a sage...

—Publilius Syrus

Wise men profit more from fools than fools from wise men; for the wise men shun the mistakes of fools, but fools do not imitate the successes of the wise... *—Marcus Cato*

A fool always finds some greater fool to admire him...
—*Nicolas Boileau*

People oppose things because they are ignorant of them...
—*El-Ghazali*

Most ignorance is vincible ignorance. We don't know because we don't want to know... —*Aldous Huxley*

Ignorant men raise questions that wise men answered thousands of years ago... —*Johann W. Goethe*

A man who has never seen the sun cannot be blamed for thinking that no glory can exceed that of the moon...
—*Calderon*

Illusions

We suffer primarily not from our vices or our weaknesses, but from our illusions. We are haunted, not by reality, but by those images we have put in place of reality...
—*Daniel J. Boorstin*

The world is an illusion, but it is an illusion which we must take seriously, because it is real as far as it goes...
—*Aldous Huxley*

The real illusion is to believe that we are separate from God...
—*Omraam M. Aivanhov*

Things are not always what they seem... —*Phaedus*

Do not hold as gold all that shines as gold...—*Allain de Lille*

Human life is an endless illusion... —*Blaise Pascal*

Pleasure can be supported by illusion, while happiness rests upon truth... —*Sebastien Chamfort*

The stripping away of illusion and the struggle to find personal reality can be likened to the peeling of an apple. As one peels away the layers of unreality...eventually only the core remains... —*Meredith L. Young*

There is no end to illusion. Life is a train of moods like a string of beads, and as we pass through them they prove to be many colored lenses which paint the world their own hue... —*Ralph W. Emerson*

Attachment is the great fabricator of illusions; reality can be attained only by someone who is detached... —*Simone Weil*

Imagination

The world is but a canvas to our imaginations... —*Henry D. Thoreau*

Imagination is our ability to see inwardly and picture there that which has not yet appeared outwardly. Imagination is God's gift to us... —*Donald Curtis*

The first power that meets us at the threshold of the Soul's domain is the power of imagination... —*Franz Hartmann*

Imagination has always had powers of resurrection that no science can match... —*Ingrid Bengis*

What is an idea? It is an image that paints itself in my brain... —*Voltaire*

A prison is never narrow when the imagination can range in it as it will... —*Marguerite of Navarre*

We are what we pretend to be, so we must be careful about what we pretend to be... —*Kurt Vonnegut*

The mind, without imagination, would be as useless as an observatory without a telescope... —*Fred Van Amburgh*

Imagination is more important than knowledge... —*Albert Einstein*

The highest and best work of imagination is the marvelous transformation that it works in character. Imagine that you are one with the Principle of good, and you will become truly good... —*Charles Fillmore*

The world of reality has its limits; the world of imagination is boundless... —*Jean J. Rousseau*

Believe that you shall receive and you shall receive...—*Jesus*

When the will and imagination are in conflict, the imagination invariably wins the day... —*Emile Coue*

Imitation

If the blind lead the blind both shall fall into the ditch... —*Jesus*

Great bodies of people are never responsible for what they do... —*Virginia Woolf*

There is a time in every man's education when he arrives at the conviction that envy is ignorance; that imitation is suicide; that he must take himself for better or worse as his portion... —*Ralph W. Emerson*

Man's natural character is to imitate; that of a sensitive man is to resemble as closely as possible the person whom he loves... —*Marquis de Sade*

Men nearly always follow the tracks made by others in their affairs by imitation... —*Niccolo Machiavelli*

He who follows another sees nothing, learns nothing, nay, seeks nothing... —*William Osler*

To admire on principle is the only way to imitate without loss of originality... —*Samuel T. Coleridge*

No man ever yet became great by imitation... —*Samuel Johnson*

Most people are other people. Their thoughts are someone else's opinions, their lives a mimicry... —*Oscar Wilde*

Immortality/Eternity

The average man, who does not know what to do with this life, wants another, one which shall last forever...

—Anatole France

Eternity is called whole, not because it has parts, but because it is lacking in nothing... *—Thomas Aquinas*

Eternity is not something that begins after you are dead. It is going on all the time. We are in it now...

—Charlotte P. Gilman

Man, tree, and flower are supposed to die; but the fact remains that God's universe is spiritual and immortal...

—Mary Baker Eddy

Expect no greater happiness in Eternity, than to rejoice in God... *—Benjamin Whichcote*

The soul of man is immortal... *—Benjamin Franklin*

Eternity is not the hereafter...This is it. If you don't get it here, you won't get it anywhere... *—Joseph Campbell*

If there is anything in me that is of permanent worth and service to the universe, the universe will know how to preserve it... *—Horace J. Bridges*

There is only one way to get ready for immortality, and that is to love this life and live it as bravely and faithfully and cheerfully as we can... *—Henry van Dyke*

Immortality is the great world of light that lies behind all human destinies... *—Henry W. Longfellow*

Journey

Do you know...Where you are...On your journey?...

—Deng Ming–Dao

Don't be afraid to take a big step if one is indicated. You can't cross a chasm in two small jumps... —*David L. George*

Whether we know it or not, we are all on a journey beyond belief... —*Roger Walsh*

If you don't see the path that meets your eye how will your feet know the way?... —*Shitou*

It is not enough to know the way; we must travel it... —*Alice H. Rice*

The distance is nothing; it is only the first step that is difficult... —*Marie A. du Deffand*

Do not follow a path. Follow your own footsteps. Your path will create itself... —*Paul Williams*

The real voyage of discovery consists not in seeking new landscapes but in seeing with new eyes... —*Marcel Proust*

The path is smooth that leadeth onto danger... —*William Shakespeare*

Not I, not anyone else, can travel that road for you. You must travel it yourself... —*Walt Whitman*

The life of man is a journey that must be traveled, however bad the roads or the accommodations... —*Oliver Goldsmith*

What we call the beginning is often the end and to make our end is to make the beginning. The end is where we start from... —*T.S. Eliot*

Wide is the gate, and broad is the way, that leads to destruction, and many there be who go that way, because straight is the gate, and narrow is the way, which leads to life, and few there be that find it... —*Jesus*

Transformation is a journey without a final destination... —*Marilyn Ferguson*

What is the path? Everyday life is the path... —*Nansen*

The first step is what counts: First beginnings are hardest to make and as small and inconspicuous as they are potent in influence, but once they are made, it is easy to add to the rest... —*Aristotle*

For thirty years I went in search of God, and when I opened my eyes at the end of this time, I discovered that it was really He who sought for me... —*Bayazid al–Bistami*

Where there is no road, a new road must be trodden...
—*Joseph Hurwitz*

Know the universe itself as a road, as many roads, as roads for traveling souls... —*Walt Whitman*

At the beginning of the spiritual path, we are like children whose only real knowledge of themselves is a reflection cast in a mirror... —*Rick Fields*

Joy

The lucky folks are the ones who get to do things they enjoy doing... —*Jerome Kern*

Real joy comes not from ease or riches or from the praise of men, but from doing something worthwhile...
—*W.T. Grenfell*

Joy is not in things, it is in us... —*Charles Wagner*

Joys are our wings; sorrows our spurs... —*Jean Paul Richter*

True enjoyment cannot be expressed in words...
—*Jean J. Rousseau*

People are always good company when they are doing what they really enjoy... —*Samuel Butler*

Great joy...is apt to be silent, and dwells rather in the heart than on the tongue... —*Henry Fielding*

Shared joy is double joy... —*Swedish proverb*

Joy is more divine than sorrow, for joy is bread and sorrow is medicine... —*Henry W. Beecher*

Joy is the feeling of grinning inside... —*Melba Colgrove*

Judgement

Judge a tree from its fruit, not from the leaves...
—*Euripides*

You should not say it is not good. You should say you do not like it, and then, you know, you're perfectly safe...
—*James M. Whistler*

We turn to using quantities when we can't compare the qualities... —*Marvin Minsky*

Judge a man by his questions rather than by his answers...
—*Voltaire*

You judge by human standards, I judge no one... —*Jesus*

The less harshly we judge ourselves, the more accepting we become of others... —*Harold Bloomfield*

No man can judge another, because no man knows himself... —*Thomas Browne*

Examine the contents of the bottle, not the bottle...
—*The Talmud*

Men are not to be judged by their looks, habits and appearances; but by the character of their lives and conversations and by their works... —*Roger L'Estrange*

Every person's map of the world is as unique as their thumbprint. There are no two people alike. No two people who understand the same sentence the same way...So in dealing with people you try not to fit them to your concept of what they should be... —*Milton Erickson*

We judge ourselves by what we feel capable of doing, while others, while others judge us by what we have already done...
—Henry W. Longfellow

We must never undervalue any person... *—Francis de Sales*

Thankfulness is an antidote to judgement...
—Michael Exeter

Judge not, and you shall not be judged; condemn not and you shall not be condemned; forgive, and you shall be forgiven... *—Jesus*

Enjoy your life without comparing it with that of others...
—Marquis de Condorcet

Kindness/Gentleness

Life is not so short but that there is always time enough for courtesy... *—Ralph W. Emerson*

Civility costs nothing and buys everything...
—Mary W. Montagu

One can always be kind to people about whom one cares nothing... *—Oscar Wilde*

Speak kindly today; when tomorrow comes you will be in practice... *—Proverb*

Kind words are the music of the world. They have a power which seems to be beyond natural causes, as if they were some angel's song which had lost its way and come to earth...
—Frederich W. Faber

Kindness is a language the dumb can speak and deaf can hear... *—Christian Bovee*

Kindness is a golden chain by which society is bound together... *—Johann W. Goethe*

Don't repay a kindness; pass it on... *—Proverb*

Let me be a little kinder, let me be a little blinder to the faults of those around me... *—Edgar A. Guest*

Laughter

Laughter is the jam on the toast of life. It adds flavor, keeps it from being too dry and makes it easier to swallow...
—Diane Johnson

The enduring love is the love that laughs...
—George J. Watham

Laughter can be more satisfying than honor; more precious than money; more heart cleansing than prayer...
—Harriet Rochlin

Jokes are an admirable instrument for reducing tensions...
—Robert Mueller

If you wish to glimpse inside a human soul and get to know a man...just watch him laugh. If he laughs well, he's a good man... *—Fyodor Dostoyevsky*

Laughter is a great soul cleanser... *—Virginia Sale*

We should tackle reality in a slightly jokey way, otherwise we miss its point... *—Lawrence Durrell*

Don't forget the recipe of making three people laugh every day... *—Edgar Cayce*

If you go to bed at night and think about your day and you haven't laughed very much, then you must jump out of bed and go do something fun... *—Marlo Morgan*

A good laugh is sunshine in a house...
—William M. Thackeray

Laughter is the brush that sweeps away the cobwebs of the heart... *—Mort Walker*

If everything goes wrong, just laugh! Just let it have its fling, let it go; but keep your vision upon God, and know that all will come right... —*White Eagle*

If you cannot laugh at yourself, do not laugh at others... —*Julie Sneyd*

Laugh and the world laughs with you; weep and you weep alone... —*Ella Wheeler Wilcox*

Laughter is a universal bond that draws all men together... —*Nathan Ausubel*

A day without laughter is a lost day... —*Robert Muller*

A man isn't poor if he can still laugh...—*Raymond Hitchcock*

Laughter is inner jogging... —*Norman Cousins*

The person who knows how to laugh at himself will never cease to be amused... —*Shirley MacLaine*

Laughter is a tranquilizer with no side effects... —*Arnold Glasow*

Lesson

Learning is a very painful experience. It requires humility from people at an age where the natural habitat is arrogance... —*May Sarton*

Love is the Law of God. You live that you may learn to love. You love that you may learn to live. No other lesson is required of man... —*Mikhail Naimy*

Every stone that bruises the pilgrim's foot will teach him a lesson. Every lesson will yield a pearl... —*Elinor MacDonald*

To learn is to change. Education is a process that changes the learner... —*George Leonard*

They can conquer who believe they can. He has not learned the first lesson of life who does not every day surmount a fear... —*Ralph W. Emerson*

Some of the best lessons we ever learn, we learn from our mistakes and failures. The error of the past is the wisdom and success of the future... —*Tryon Edwards*

The lesson that most of us on this voyage never learn, but can never quite forget, is that to win is sometimes to lose... —*Richard M. Nixon*

Our bravest and best lessons are not learned through success, but through misadventure... —*Amos B. Alcott*

There is no shortcut to life. To the end of our days, life is a lesson imperfectly learned... —*Harrison E. Salisbury*

Life

Life is a gift from God, an unlimited series of opportunities to find the good in ourselves and others. There is good in everything, if we are willing to see it... —*Alan Cohen*

Life is the only game where the object of the game is to figure out what the rules are... —*Tom Seeley*

Life is made of marble and mud... —*Nathaniel Hawthorne*

Life is full of giving and taking. If the giving is more than the taking, then by just that much the individual rises towards a higher life... —*Julian P. Johnson*

Life is a bridge. Cross over it, but build no house on it... —*American Indian proverb*

We are always getting ready to live, but never living... —*Ralph W. Emerson*

When you're not afraid to die, life becomes much more meaningful... —*Barbara Harris*

Life seems to be a series of crises that have to be faced...
—Helen Hayes

Life is not about limitation, it's about options...
—Brooke Knapp

Life just is. You have to flow with it. Give yourself to the moment. Let it happen... *—Jerry Brown*

Life is really simple. What we give out, we get back...
—Louise L. Hay

All the world's a stage, and all the men and women merely players; they have their entrances and exits; and one man in his time has many parts... *—William Shakespeare*

Love says: "I am everything." Wisdom says: "I am nothing." Between the two my life flows... *—Jack Kornfield*

Life's supreme adventure is the adventure of living. Life's greatest achievement is the continual remaking of yourself so at last you do know how to live... *—Winfred Rhodes*

Life is too brief to waste even one moment in useless regret or vain expectation... *—Dorothy Strange*

Life is a glass given us to fill... *—William A. Brown*

Only a life lived for others is a life worthwhile...
—Albert Einstein

Life is a flower of which love is the honey... *—Victor Hugo*

I have found that if you love life, life will love you back...
—Arthur Rubinstein

Life is a one–way, its law is the same for all, it moves only forwards... *—Paul Tournier*

Life is a series of surprises... *—Ralph W. Emerson*

Life is a dream for the wise, a game for the fool, a comedy for the rich, a tragedy for the poor... *—Shalom Aleichem*

Life is not first lived and then understood; it is poorly lived till understood... —*George A. Gordon*

The true meaning of life is to plant trees, under whose shade you do not expect to sit... —*Nelson Henderson*

The mystery of life is that everybody dies, but nobody believes they will. It's only when we understand and accept this inevitability that we really begin living... —*Bernie Siegal*

The aim of life is to live, and to live means to be aware, joyously, drunkenly, serenely, divinely aware...

—*Henry Miller*

The meaning of life is the road, not the goal...

—*Arthur Schnitzler*

Life is what happens while we're busy making other plans...

—*John Lennon*

Life is a long preparation for something that never happens...

—*William B. Yeats*

Life is not truly Life while the thought of death can still disturb it... —*Karlfried G. Durckheim*

Every man's life is a fairy tale, written by God's fingers...

—*Hans Christian Andersen*

Life is really simple, but men insist on making it complicated... —*Confucius*

There are two ways to slice easily through life: to believe everything or to doubt everything. Both ways save us from thinking... —*Alfred Korzybski*

It's a funny thing about life; if you refuse to accept anything but the best, you very often get it... —*Somerset Maugham*

Life holds no mystery. From the very beginning, as man of today understands the beginning, life has been complete. There is nothing man can add to life, but there is much for man to enjoy... —*Frater Achad*

The whole world is a comedy to those that think, a tragedy to those that feel... —*Horace Walpole*

If you harvest the strength to impose your own terms upon life, you must accept the terms it offers you... —*T.S. Eliot*

There must be more to life than having everything... —*Maurice Sendak*

Life is an error–making and error–correcting process... —*Jonas Salk*

Accept every event in your life as natural, whether it is life, death, birth, marriage, goings or comings. Accept everyone. Do not argue. Do not question. Do not doubt. Do not judge. You will find that each step will lead on to another one, and when you start living this way there will be a great rejoicing in the heavens because a prodigal son or daughter is beginning to return home... —*Ronald Beesley*

Life is neither a good or an evil; it is simply a place where good and evil exist... —*Seneca*

The principal business of life is to enjoy it...—*Samuel Butler*

I count all that part of my life lost which I spend not in communion with God, or in doing good... —*John Danne*

Life is like a library owned by an author. In it are a few books which he wrote himself, but most of them were written for him... —*Harry E. Fosdick*

Light

Experience is a dim light, which only lights the one who bears it... —*Louis–Ferdinand Celiné*

The greater the darkness, the more power the light has by contrast. If you light a candle in a totally darkened room, the candle has an almost shattering effect upon the darkness... —*Ron Watson*

Truly, it is in darkness that one finds the light, so when we are in sorrow, then this light is nearest to all of us...

—*Meister Eckhart*

There are two ways of spreading light: to be the candle or the mirror that reflects it... —*Edith Wharton*

Keep your face to the sunshine and you cannot see the shadow... —*Helen Keller*

A sensible man would remember that the eyes may be confused in two ways, and for two resons—by a change from light to darkness, or from darkness to light. He will consider that the same will happen with the soul... —*Plato*

It is better to light one small candle than to curse the darkness... —*Confucius*

There is no object so foul that intense light will not make it beautiful... —*Ralph W. Emerson*

Give light and the darkness will disappear of itself...

—*Erasmus*

When you think everything is hopeless, a little ray of light comes from somewhere... —*German proverb*

There is not enough darkness in all the world to put out the light of even one small candle... —*Robert Alden*

A light for one is a light for a hundred... —*The Talmud*

Let the light penetrate the darkness until the darkness shines and there is no longer any division between the two...

—*Hebrew proverb*

Only the light which we have kindled in ourselves can illuminate others... —*Arthur Schopenhauer*

Light, even though it passes through pollution, is not polluted... —*Augustine*

Little

Little drops of water, little grains of sand, make the mighty ocean and the pleasant land... —*Julia A. Fletcher Carney*

Practice yourself, for heaven's sake, in little things; and thence proceed to greater... —*Epictetus*

Most of the critical things in life, which become the starting points of human destiny, are little things... —*Robert Smith*

Small deeds done are better than great deeds planned... —*Peter Marshall*

Too often we underestimate the power of a touch, a smile, a kind work, a listening ear, an honest compliment, or the smallest act of caring, all of which has the potential to turn a life around... —*Leo Buscaglia*

Drop by drop, the measure is filled... —*Old Testament*

Has the thought ever struck your intellectual roundhouse that life is made up of little things—that quiet people who are always doing the little things often accomplish the most... —*Fred Van Amburgh*

The things that count most in life are usually the little things that cannot be counted... —*Bernard Meltzer*

Little things are indeed little, but to be faithful in little things is a great thing... —*Augustine*

Big doesn't necessarily mean better. Sunflowers aren't better than violets... —*Edna Ferber*

It is the greatest of all mistakes to do nothing because you can only do little. Do what you can... —*Sydney Smith*

Little by little does the trick... —*Aesop*

The beginnings of all things are small... —*Cicero*

We shut our eyes to the beginnings of evil because they are small, and in this weakness lies the germ of our defeat...
—Henri F. Amiel

Loneliness

The person who tries to live alone will not succeed as a human being. His heart withers if he doesn't answer another heart. His mind shrinks away if he hears only the echoes of his own thoughts and finds no other inspiration...
—Pearl Buck

Man's loneliness is but his fear of life... *—Eugene O'Neill*

Man is never alone...His existence and feelings are individual and collective at one and same time... *—Eliphas Levi*

What loneliness is more lonely than distrust?...
—George Eliot

In cities, no one is quiet but many are lonely; in the country, people are quiet but few are lonely... *—Geoffrey F. Fisher*

Are you lonely, O my brother? Share your little hand with another! Stretch your hand to one unfriended and your loneliness is ended... *—John Oxenham*

The worst loneliness is not to be comfortable with yourself...
—Mark Twain

There is no loneliness if one is satisfied with oneself...
—Hans–Ulrich Rieker

There is none more lonely than the man who loves only himself... *—Abraham Ibn Esra*

Loneliness is the way by which destiny endeavors to lead man to himself... *—Hermann Hesse*

Loneliness vanishes completely in the stillness...
—Paul Brunton

Love

Love is the great solvent of all difficulties, all problems, all misunderstandings...
—White Eagle

Love is greater than faith, because the end is greater than the means...(Love) is greater than charity, again, because the whole is greater than the part...
—Henry Drummond

To love is to place our happiness in the happiness of another...
—Gottfried Leibnitz

When we love, we see the infinite in the finite. We find the Creator in the creation...True love is a dazzling revelation of the immortality of the soul...
—Eliphas Levi

If love does not know how to give and take without restrictions, it is not love, but a transaction that never fails to lay stress on a plus and a minus...
—Emma Goldman

When we love, we lose ourselves, and conversely when we have lost ourselves...we become capable of inexhaustible love...
—Stephen Larsen

The only way you can ever hope to be loved is to stop asking for it and start giving it; you get love only when you give it to others...
—Dale Carnegie

They do not love who do not show their love...
—William Shakespeare

Only love can be divided endlessly and still not diminish...
—Anne Morrow Lindbergh

When we come to the last moment of this lifetime, and we look back across it, the only thing that's going to matter is "What was the quality of our love?"...
—Richard Bach

There is no right or wrong. There is only love...
—Carol Chapman

The conclusion is always the same: love is the most powerful and still the most unknown energy of the world...

—*Teilhard de Chardin*

It is possible that a man can be so changed by love as hardly to be recognized as the same person... —*Terence*

Don't fall into the trap that there is only one special person that you are able to love. Instead, try to develop the expectation that the world is full of people that you can love and that can love you... —*Ken Keyes, Jr.*

Love is the power of God that binds two souls and makes them one; there is no power on earth that can dissolve that bond... —*The Aquarian Gospel*

In real love you want the other person's good. In romantic love you want the other person... —*Margaret Anderson*

Love has no errors, for all errors are the want of love...

—*William Law*

Love is but the discovery of ourselves in others, and the delight in the recognition... —*Alexander Smith*

Love does not survive neglect. Once planted, it must be carefully tended if it is to grow... —*Alice H. Rice*

Love, the magician, knows this little trick whereby two people walk in different directions yet always remain side by side...

—*Hugh Prather*

Perfect love means to love the one through whom one becomes happy... —*Sören Kierkegaard*

When love comes, reason flees hastily away...

—*Ferid Ed–dim Attar*

Love one human being purely and warmly, and you will love all... —*Jean Paul Richter*

Love cures. It cures those who give it and it cures those who receive it... —*Karl A. Menninger*

The only genuine love worthy of the name is unconditional... —*John Powell*

Love makes every space sacred and every moment meaningful... —*Barbara De Angelis*

We don't love qualities, we love persons, sometimes by reason of their defects as well as their qualities... —*Jacques Maritain*

One word frees us of all the weight and pain of life: that word is love... —*Sophocles*

When love and skill work together, expect a masterpiece... —*John Ruskin*

Love cannot stay at home; a man cannot keep it to himself. Like light, it is constantly traveling. A man must spend it, must give it away... —*Alexander Macleod*

Love doesn't make the world go 'round. Love is what makes the ride worthwhile... —*Franklin P. Jones*

People who do not experience self love have little or no capacity to love others... —*Nathaniel Branden*

Love is space and time measured by the heart... —*Marcel Proust*

Love is an act of endless forgiveness... —*Peter Ustinov*

Love is when each person is more concerned for the other than for one's self... —*David Frost*

If you would be loved, love and be lovable... —*Benjamin Franklin*

In love, respect should come first and ardor second... —*Robert Benson*

Love turns one person into two; and two into one...
—Isaac Abravanel

Love requires no defense and bears no need to prove itself. It knows that it is lovable, and all that comes from love must be lovable, too... *—Alan Cohen*

Love brings to life whatever is dead around us...
—Franz Rosenzweig

Love does not make you weak because it is the source of all strength, but it makes you see the nothingness of the illusionary strength on which you depended before you knew it... *—Leon Bloy*

Love rules without rules... *—Italian saying*

Love is the holy bond that holds all worlds together...
—Julian P. Johnson

The love we give away is the only love we keep...
—Elbert Hubbard

A man doesn't learn to understand anything unless he loves it... *—Johann W. Goethe*

True love demands nothing, seeks nothing for its own, but desires only to give. If we love God and our neighbor we desire only to give, to serve, to pour out all that we have at the feet of life... *—Henry T. Hamblin*

I will love you no matter what. I will love you if you are stupid, if you slip and fall on your face, if you do the wrong thing, if you make mistakes, if you behave like a human being—I will love you no matter what... *—Leo Buscaglia*

As a human being related to all living beings, we must be first related to ourselves. We cannot understand, love and welcome others without first knowing and loving ourselves...
—Jean Klein

Love makes all hard hearts gentle... —*George Herbert*

Love is the biggest eraser there is. Love erases even the deepest imprinting because love goes deeper than anything...
—*Louise Hayes*

If God is love, the more we can understand the nature of love and put that understanding into practice, the more God–like will be our experience... —*Reginald Armor*

Love is not blind. Lust is blind. If love is blind, God is blind...
—*Gordon Palmer*

Love is the reduction of the universe to a single being...
—*Victor Hugo*

Meditation

Meditation provides a way of learning how to let go. As we sit, the self we've been trying to construct and make into a nice, neat package continues to unravel... —*John Welwood*

Meditation helps keep us from identifying with the "movies of the mind."... —*Joan Borysenko*

Meditation is that exercise of the mind by which it recalls a known truth... —*George Horne*

Meditation is a valuable exercise, but eventually you have to open up your eyes and look around... —*Dan Millman*

Prayer is speaking to God. Meditation is listening. Trust tranquility... —*Shirley MacLaine*

A meditator keeps his mind open every second. He is constantly investigating life, investigating his own experience, viewing existence in a detached and inquisitive way. Thus, he is constantly open to truth in any form, from any source, and at any time... —*Henepola Gunartana*

There is no necessity for a technique or formula for meditation. Inner feeling, or inner knowing, is the Silent Voice of inspiration... —*Walter Russell*

Mind

I find, by experience, that the mind and the body are more than married, for they are most intimately united; and when one suffers, the other sympathizes... —*Philip Chesterfield*

The beginning of wisdom is to know the imperfection of one's own mind. If a man recognizes its weakness, he will not use it as a means to answer important questions...

—*Epictetus*

The human mind...is incapable of thinking rightly. It thinks from the point of view of error and limitation, instead of from the point of view of Truth and limitless power...In order to be free one must reverse his thouthts, learning to think from the Universal Mind, instead of from the finite mind... —*Henry T. Hamblin*

Where there is an open mind, there will always be a frontier... —*Charles Kettering*

Man's mind stretched by a new idea never goes back to its original dimension... —*Oliver W. Holmes*

We are caught in the prison of the mind. If we are to escape we must recognize that we are in prison. If we think we are free, then no escape is possible... —*George I. Gurdjieff*

Small minds cannot handle great themes... —*St. Jerome*

Our minds have unbelievable power over our bodies...

—*André Maurois*

Empty your mind. Become still, and everything will happen of its own accord. There is really nothing you have to do. Just be still... —*Robert Adams*

Great minds have purpose; others have wishes. Little minds are tamed and subdued by misfortunes, but great minds rise above them... —*Washington Irving*

The causes of all poverty are in the mind, and when these are removed abundance fills the life to overflowing. This does not mean the acquisition of great wealth, but something far better in every way... —*Henry T. Hamblin*

The immature mind hops from one thing to another; the mature mind seeks to follow through...—*Harry A. Overstreet*

Our minds are like our stomachs, they are whetted by the change of their food, and variety supplies both with fresh appetite... —*Quintilian*

The mind's highest good is the knowledge of God, and the mind's highest virtue is to know God... —*Baruch Spinoza*

A closed mind is a dying mind... —*Edna Ferber*

Our minds are like crows. They pick up everything that glitters, no matter how uncomfortable our nests get with all that metal in them... —*Thomas Merton*

The mind is a dangerous weapon, even to the possessor, if he knows not discreetly how to use it... —*Michel Montaigne*

If your mind is empty, it is always ready for anything; it is open to everything. In the beginner's mind there are many possibilities; in the expert's mind there are few...
—*Shunryu Suzuki*

Man's mind is his essence; he is where his thoughts are...
—*Nahman Bratzlav*

The function of the mind is thinking; when you think, you keep your mind, and when you don't think, you lose your mind...That is how a man becomes a great man...
—*Mencius*

Minds are not conquered by force, but by love and highmindedness... —*Baruch Spinoza*

The mind is a useful servant, but a very bad master... —*Julian P. Johnson*

The sound body is a product of the sound mind... —*George B. Shaw*

The husbandman deals with land; physicians and trainers with the body; the wise man with his own Mind...—*Epictetus*

Make up your mind you can't—and you're always right... —*Bob Goddard*

Miracles

A miracle is what happens when you are going from one point to another in your life and suddenly you are at your destination without taking what you thought were the necessary steps... —*Ron Smothermon*

True miracles are created by men when they use the courage and intelligence that God gave them... —*Jean Anouilh*

There are only two ways to live your life. One is as though nothing is a miracle. The other is as though everything is a miracle... —*Albert Einstein*

To aim to convert a man by miracles is a profanation of the soul... —*Ralph W. Emerson*

The place where light and dark begin to touch is where miracles arise... —*Robert A. Johnson*

We are miracles. Each of us is an absolute astonishment. So whether you believe in miracles or not, we still are. We still partake of "miracledom."... —*Ruby Doe*

Miracles are signs not to them that believe, but to them that disbelieve... —*Thomas Aquinas*

If angels come not to minister unto us it is because we do not invite them, it is because we keep the door closed through which they might otherwise enter...

—*Ralph W. Trine*

A miracle is never lost. It may touch many people you have not even met, and produce undreamed changes in situations of which you are not even aware...

—*A Course In Miracles*

Moderation

Everything that exceeds the bounds of moderation has an unstable foundation... —*Seneca*

A man can find satisfaction with enough... —*Keri Hulme*

If a man oversteps the limits of moderation, he pollutes his body and mind. To be god–like is to be natural; to be natural is to follow Nature...(i.e., to keep) within the limits set by instinct and reason... —*Inazo Nitobe*

Non violent extremes endure; a sober moderation stands secure... —*Charles Alleyn*

He knows to live who keeps the middle state..

—*Alexander Pope*

The true boundary of man is moderation...

—*Owen Felltham*

Keep the golden mean between saying too much and too little... —*Publilius Syrus*

Money

Money is a wonderful thing, but it is possible to pay too high a price for it... —*Alexander Bloch*

The poorest man in the world is he who has nothing but money... —*John D. Rockefeller*

Where there is money, there is fighting...
—*Marian Anderson*

For money, people sell their soul... —*Sophocles*

As long as money is our servant it works for us, the moment it becomes master we work for it... — *Alice H. Rice*

Money attracts egotism and irresistibly leads to its misuse...
—*Albert Einstein*

Money can buy the husk of things, but not the kernel. It brings you food but not appetite, medicine but not health, acquaintances but not friends, servants but not faithfulness, days of joy but not peace or happiness... —*Henrik Ibsen*

It's good to have money and the things that money can buy, but it's good, too, to check up once in a while and make sure you haven't lost the things that money can't buy...
—*George H. Lorimer*

I can't afford to waste my time making money...
—*Louis Agassiz*

If someone thinks that when he or she makes a million dollars, he or she will be happy, that person is a very great fool... —*Leo Buscaglia*

The love of money is the mother of all evil... —*Phocylides*

Money never made a man happy yet, nor will it. There is nothing in its nature to produce happiness. The more a man has, the more he wants. Instead of filling a vacuum, it makes one... —*Benjamin Franklin*

The darkest hour of any man's life is when he sits down to plan how to get money without earning it...—*Horace Greeley*

If money is your hope for independence you will never have it. The only real security that a man can have in the world is a reserve of knowledge, experience, and ability...
—*Henry Ford*

Nature

Man masters nature not by force but by understanding...
—*Jacob Bronowski*

Nature is a volume of what God is the author...
—*Moses Harvey*

In nature nothing creates itself and nothing destroys itself...
—*Maria Montessori*

We do not see nature with our eyes, but with our understanding and our hearts... —*William Hazlitt*

Repetition is the only form of permanence that nature can achieve... —*George Santayana*

Nature is one grand cosmic book describing the power and majesty of God... —*John A. O'Brien*

There is no other door to knowledge than the door nature opens; there is no other truth except the truths we discover in nature... —*Luther Burbank*

Nature always takes her time. Great oaks don't become great overnight. They also lose a lot of leaves, branches and bark in the process of becoming great... —*Andrew Matthews*

He who understands nature walks with God...—*Edgar Cayce*

If I were to name the three most precious resources of life, I would say books, friends and nature; and the greatest of these, at least the most constant and always at hand, is nature... —*John Burroughs*

Nature has no beginning and no end. Everything in it acts upon everything else, everything is relative, everything is at

once effect and cause, acting and reacting on all sides...
—*Ludwig Feuerbach*

Nature never deceives us; it is always we who deceive ourselves... —*Jean J. Rousseau*

Nature gives to every time and season some beauties of its own; and from morning to night, as from the cradle to the grave, is a succession of changes so gentle and easy we can scarcely mark their progress... —*Charles Dickens*

Nature cannot be hastened. The bloom of a flower opens in its own proper time... —*Paul Brunton*

Nothing/Emptiness

God made everything out of nothing... —*Paul Valery*

The truth is that everything and nothing are the same and that we are both. You are not your body and your body is contained within you... —*Ron Smothermon*

Nothing is void of God; He Himself fills his work... —*Seneca*

When nothing is sure, everything is possible...
—*Margaret Drabble*

Death and emptiness are the firm ground upon which life walks... —*Alan Watts*

Only when we are nothing do we become everything...
—*Nancy D. Potts*

Born from nothingness, man goes back to nothingness...
—*Seneca*

Ideas come from space. This may seem astonishing and impossible to believe, but it is true. Ideas come from out of space... —*Thomas Edison*

Emptiness is perhaps the greatest wealth one can possess, for it provides the arena for adventure, discovery and creativity... —*Peter Oppenheimer*

Positively, the best thing a man can do is nothing, and, next to that, perhaps, good works... —*Charles Lamb*

He is nowhere who is everywhere... —*Seneca*

Nothingness is the building blocks of the universe...
—*J. A. Wheeler*

Everything is emptiness and form is condensed emptiness...
—*Albert Einstein*

Things are entirely what they appear to be—and behind them...there is nothing... —*Jean Paul Sartre*

Old Age

We grow old as soon as we cease to love and trust...
—*Louise H. de Choiseul*

The worst thing about being seventy–five years old is being treated as a seventy–five years old... —*Norman Cousins*

Up to one's last breath, one may retain the simple joys of childhood, the poetic ecstasies of the young man, the enthusiasms of maturity. Right to the end, one may intoxicate one's spirit with flowers, with beauty and with smiles... —*Eliphas Levi*

The objective is to live a full life, not just a long one. Survival into old age requires only good luck, whereas living enough demands character... —*Seneca*

We age, not by years, but by events and our emotional reactions to them... —*Arnold A. Hutschnecker*

A man is not old until regrets take the place of dreams...
—*John Barrymore*

When a man acts wisely, he grows old slowly. When he acts

unwisely, he grows older and older every day and in every way... —*Fred Van Amburgh*

Old age is not a time of life. It is a condition of the body. It is not time that ages the body, it is abuse that does...
—*Herbert M. Shelton*

Old age is the climbing of a mountain. The higher you get, the more tired and breathless you become. But your view becomes much more extensive... —*Ingmar Bergman*

To know how to grow old is a masterpiece of wisdom, and one of the most difficult chapters in the great art of living...
—*Henri F. Amiel*

Age does not depend upon years, but upon temperament and health. Some men are born old and some men grow so... —*Tryon Edwards*

Each part of life has its own pleasures. Each has its own abundant harvest, to be garnered in season. We may grow old in body, but we need never grow old in mind and spirit...No one is as old as to think he cannot live one more year... —*Cicero*

Young souls look for happiness, older ones for peace, calm, and equilibrium... —*Paul Brunton*

If wrinkles must be written upon our brows, let them not be written upon the heart. The spirit should not grow old...
—*James Garfield*

When one finds company in himself and his pursuits he cannot feel old, no matter what his years may be...
—*Amos B. Alcott*

Those who love deeply never grow old; they might die of old age, but they die young... —*Arthur W. Pinero*

Anyone who keeps the ability to see beauty never grows old...
—*Franz Kafka*

For the man who has lived for the body, old age is decay; for the man who has lived for the spirit it is an apotheosis (exaltation)... —*Jean Delay*

I used to think that eighty was a very old age, but now that I am ninety–one I don't think so any more. There are times I feel like a boy. As long as you are able to admire and to love, you are young... —*Pablo Casals*

That man never grows old who keeps a child in his heart... —*Richard Steele*

The older I grow, the more apt I am to doubt my own judgement and to pay more respect to the judgement of others... —*Benjamin Franklin*

Let your old age be childlike, and your childhood like old age; that is, so that neither may your wisdom be with pride, nor your humility without wisdom... —*Augustine*

Oneness

There is no boundary between subject and object, self and no–self, seer and seen...the subject an object always turn out to be one... —*Ken Wilber*

In the deeper reality beyond space and time, we may be all members of one body... —*James Jeans*

All things are connected like to blood that connects us all. Man did not weave the web of life, he is merely a strand in it... —*Chief Seattle*

Everything in the universe is connected, everything is osmosis. You cannot separate any part from the whole; interdependence rules the cosmic order... —*Taisen Deshimaru*

Life and death are one, even as the river and the sea are one... —*Kahlil Gibran*

The true doctrine of omnipresence is that God reappears with all His parts in every moss and cobweb...

—*Ralph W. Emerson*

Survival is the second law of life. The first is that we are all one...
—*Joseph Campbell*

We are members of one great body... —*Seneca*

There is one truth and one goodness penetrating and governing all things... —*Giordano Bruno*

All creatures seek after unity; all multiplicity struggles toward it—the universal aim of all life is always this unity...

—*Johannes Tauler*

Do you think that God is only in your heart? You should be able to recognize Him in every garden, in every forest, in every house, and in every person... —*Shems Tabriez*

Realize that each soul is related to you. When you recognize that everyone is part of you, you will find you cannot withdraw from another... —*Elsie Morgan*

All souls are one. Each is a spark of the original soul, and this soul is inherent in all souls... —*Hasidic saying*

The chain which makes us one, is to honor the one God...

—*Philo*

Unity is convertible with eternity, for there cannot be more than one Eternal God... —*Nicholas of Cusa*

There is no man alone, because every man is a microcosm, and carries the whole world about him... —*Thomas Browne*

The moment a person realizes his oneness with the Infinite Spirit he recognizes himself as a spiritual being, and no longer a physical, material being... —*Ralph W. Trine*

Order

There is no chance, and no anarchy in the universe. All is system and gradation. Every god is there sitting in his sphere...
—*Ralph W. Emerson*

Order is heaven's first law... —*Alexander Pope*

Order means light and peace, inward liberty and free command over one's self; order is power...—*Henri F. Amiel*

Every man is where he is by the law of his being; the thoughts which he has built into his character have brought him there, and in the arrangement of his life there is no element of chance... —*James Allen*

Good order is the foundation of all things...
—*Edmund Burke*

Order is the sanity of the mind, the health of the body, the peace of the city, the security of the state. As the beams to a house, as the bones to a body, so is order to all things...
—*Robert Southey*

Any power capable of creating the world and overseeing the orderly process of evolution must know exactly where it is going and how it intends to get there. Its course cannot possibily be altered by any one of the finite minds it has created... —*U S. Anderson*

It is a rare life that remains orderly even in private...
—*Michel Montaigne*

Beauty is absent where order is lacking... —*Philo*

Pain

The cup of pain, though it burns your lips, has been fashioned from the clay which the potter has moistened with his own sacred tears... —*Arabian saying*

Pain is no longer pain when it is past... —*Margaret Preston*

The means by which certain pleasures are gained brings pains many times greater than the pleasures... —*Epicurus*

So long as you can sweeten another's pain, life is not in vain... —*Helen Keller*

The purpose of pain is not to punish but to teach... —*Elinor MacDonald*

We are a feelingless people. If we could really feel, the pain would be so great that we would stop all the suffering... —*Julian Beck*

The whole purpose of letting pain be pain is precisely this: to let go of pain. By entering into it, we see that we are strong enough and capable enough to move through it. We find out that it ultimately has a gift for us... —*Matthew Fox*

There is no pain quite like that of a broken heart. But a broken heart is an open heart. When we allow ourselves to to be broken, a gentle transformation takes place... —*Douglas Bloch*

Pain confers spiritual insight, a beauty of outlook, a philosophy of life... —*Louis E. Bisch*

One of the greatest pains to human nature is the pain of a new idea... —*Walter Bagehot*

Change is painful when we attach our happiness to outer circumstances... —*Jesse Jennings*

Pain is neither intolerable nor everlasting...It is the power of the soul to maintain its own serenity... —*David Grayson*

Pain is telling us something is wrong, that we need to behave differently, that what hurts must be fixed... —*Ernie Larson*

Your pain is the breaking of the shell that encloses your understanding... —*Kahlil Gibran*

Past

In the carriages of the past you can't go anywhere... —*Maxim Gorky*

What is done, is done... —*William Shakespeare*

Rather than cursing the past, bless it... —*Wayne Dyer*

Why wish for the privilege of living your past life again? You begin a new one every morning... —*Robert Quillen*

God has no power over the past except to cover it with oblivion... —*Pliny the Elder*

The past is present in the future... —*Louis L. Mann*

Regrets are caused by a misuse of memory...The man who broods over the past can never master the difficulties of today. Every wise man learns to forget. He does not allow himself to become a slave to his memory... —*Herbert Casson*

Rather than cursing the past, bless it... —*Wayne Dyer*

Why wish for the privilege of living your past life again? You begin a new one every morning... —*Robert Quillen*

No man having put his hand to the plow and looking back is fit for the kingdom of heaven... —*Jesus*

You can never plan the future by the past... —*Edmund Burke*

A good memory is one trained to forget the trivial... —*Clifton Fadiman*

Look at the past like a bullet. Once it's fired it's finished... —*Catherine Bauby*

We crucify ourselves between two thieves: regret for yesterday and fear of tomorrow... —*Fulton Oursler*

Patience

Flowers do not force their way with great strife. Flowers open to perfection slowly in the sun...Don't be in a hurry about spiritual matters. Go step by step, and be very sure...
—*White Eagle*

The first proof of a well–ordered mind is to be able to pause and linger with itself... —*Seneca*

There is no way to push the river; equally you cannot hasten the harvest... —*Ralph Blum*

The philosophy of waiting is sustained by all the oracles of the universe... —*Ralph W. Emerson*

There is as much difference between genuine patience and sullen endurance, as between the smile of love, and the malicious gnashing of the teeth... —*William S. Plumer*

Patience is the best remedy for every trouble... —*Plautus*

We shall sooner have the fowl by hatching the egg than by smashing it... —*Abraham Lincoln*

The slower you go, the farther you will be...
—*Russian proverb*

Everything comes if a man will only wait... —*Tancred*

There is no great achievement that is not the result of patient working and waiting... —*Josiah Holland*

Stumbling is the fruit of haste... —*Arabian saying*

To go faster, you must slow down... —*John Brunner*

To know how to wait is the great secret of success...
—*Xavier de Maistre*

Patience can't be acquired overnight. It is just like building

up a muscle. Every day you need to work on it...
—Eknath Easwaran

Patience is a gift that God only gives to those He loves...
—African proverb

Only those who have the patience to do simple things perfectly will acquire the skill to do difficult things easily...
—Johann von Schiller

There is nothing so bitter, that a patient mind cannot find some solace for it... *—Seneca*

If I were asked what single qualification was necessary for one who has care of children, I should say patience—patience with their tempers, with their understandings, with their progress... *—Francois Fenelon*

All things come round to him who will but wait...
—Henry W. Longfellow

Of all the qualities of an excellent character, patience is enough for us... *—Michel Montaigne*

Our patience will achieve more than our force...
—Edmund Burke

A man who is master of patience is master of everything else... *—Lord Halifax*

The greater our hurry, the longer the way; the greater our patience, the sooner we reach the goal... *—German proverb*

Peace/Harmony

At the heart of the cyclone tearing the sky...is a place of central calm... *—Edwin Markham*

For peace of mind, resign as general manager of the universe... *—Larry Eiseberg*

Peace is a costly privilege—to be fought for, attained and

won. It comes only from a conquered mind...

—*Paul Brunton*

Harmony seldom makes a headline... —*Silas Bent*

We should have much peace if we would not busy ourselves with the sayings and doings of others... —*Thomas à Kempis*

Discord is rife in the outward world, but unbroken harmony holds sway at the heart of the universe... —*James Allen*

Like water, we are truest to our nature in repose...

—*Cyril Connolly*

What is dangerous about tranquilizers is that whatever peace of mind they bring is packaged peace of mind. When you buy a pill and buy peace with it, you get conditioned to cheap solutions instead of deep ones... —*Max Lerner*

In the gates of eternity the black hand and the white hand hold each other with equal clasp... —*Harriet Beecher Stowe*

Never be in a hurry; do everything quietly and in a calm spirit. Do not lose your inward peace for anything whatsoever, even if your whole world seems upset...

—*Francis de Sales*

Where there is peace and meditation, then there is neither anxiety nor doubt... —*Francis of Assisi*

When everything is in its right place within us, we ourselves are in balance with the whole work of God...

—*Henry F. Amiel*

If you really want peace of mind and inner calm, you will get it. Regardless of how unjustly you have been treated, or how unfair the boss has been, or what a mean scoundrel someone has proved to be, all this makes no difference to you when you awaken to your mental and spiritual powers...

—*Joseph Murphy*

Nothing can bring you peace but yourself. Nothing can bring you peace but the triumph of principles...

—*Ralph W. Emerson*

Peace rules the day where reason rules the mind...

—*Wilkie Collins*

Five great enemies to peace inhabit us: avarice, ambition, envy, anger and pride. If those enemies were to be banished, we would infallibly enjoy perpetual peace...

—*Petrarch*

When a man finds no peace within himself it is useless to seek it elsewhere... —*Francois La Rochefoucauld*

If you only knew the peace there is in accepted sorrow...

—*Madame Guyon*

Our work for peace must begin within the private world of each of us... —*Dag Hammarskjöld*

The first rule is to keep an untroubled spirit. The second is to look things in the face and know them for what they are...

—*Marcus Aurelius*

There can never be peace between nations until there is first known that true peace which...is within the souls of men... —*Black Elk*

Peace cannot be kept by force. It can only be achieved by understanding... —*Albert Einstein*

Perfection

Everything has its own perfection, be it higher or lower in the scale of things; and the perfection of one is not the

perfection of another... —*John H. Newman*

No one ever approaches perfection except by stealth, and unknown to themselves... —*William Hazlitt*

This is the very perfection of man, to find out his own perfection... —*Augustine*

If we accept God as perfect, we must admit a perfect universe and Cosmic scheme. If, however, we do not accept a belief in a perfect universe, then we have to accept an imperfect Creator... —*Henry T. Hamblin*

We are part of a design which fits all its parts together perfectly... —*C. Alan Anderson*

Be ye perfect, even as your Father which is in Heaven is perfect... —*Jesus*

Perfection consists not in doing extraordinary things, but in doing ordinary things extraordinarily well. Neglect nothing, the most trivial action may be performed to God...
—*Angelique Arnauld*

If you consistently do your best, the worst won't happen...
—*B. C. Forbes*

When you aim for perfection, you discover it's a moving target... —*George Fisher*

Perfection consists in one thing alone, which is doing the will of God... —*Vincent de Paul*

When a thing bores you, do not do it. Do not pursue fruitless perfection... —*Eugene Delacroix*

Perfection...of all the ways to reach it, the first is humility; the second is humility; the third, humility... —*Augustine*

The image of perfection is the sun and if you adapt him as your model, if, like him, you think of nothing but bringing light, warmth and life to all creatures, then you will really work your own transformation... —*Omraam M. Aivanhov*

Perseverance

We have many second chances in life, sometimes even tenth chances. Let no man give up hope till the last breath is drawn... —*Charles F. Potter*

The difference between perseverance and obstinacy is that one comes from a strong will and the other from a strong won't... —*Henry W. Beecher*

Do not be afraid to demand great things of yourself. Powers which you never dreamed you possessed will leap to your assistance... —*Orison S. Marden*

In the confrontation between the stream and the rock, the stream always wins—not through strength but by perseverance... —*H. Jackson Brown*

Continuous effort—not strength or intelligence–is the key to unlocking our potential... —*Liane Cordes*

The drops of rain make a hole in the stone, not by violence, but by often falling... —*Lucretius*

Great people are just ordinary people with an extraordinary amount of determination... —*Robert Schuller*

I think and think for months and years. Ninety nine times the conclusion is false. The hundredth time I am right... —*Albert Einstein*

There is no royal road to anything. One thing at a time, and all things in succession. That which grows slowly, endures... —*Josiah Holland*

Persistent people begin their success where others end in failure... —*Edward Eggleston*

Persistence has performed greater things than ambition and ability. If you lack persistency where you are, you will lack grit where you go... —*Fred Van Amburgh*

Victory belongs to the most persevering...
—Napoleon Bonaparte

We will either find a way or make one... *—Hannibal*

Success depends upon staying power. The reason for failure in most cases is lack of perseverance...
—James R. Miller

The man who persists in knocking will succeed in entering...
—Moses Ibn Ezra

Pessimism

The pessimist tells us that the thorns outlive the roses, and this is true, but a sharp prick from a thorn teaches us to use more care in gathering roses... *—Fred Van Amburgh*

When people are depressed they are also pessimistic...
—Martin E.P. Seligman

I never think of the negative. All obstacles can be overcome...
—Donald Trump

You can't raise positive people on negative feedback...
—Gerald Jampolsky

Pessimists are second–rate people. They do not believe in life. Pessimism is just an excuse for their cowardice. All they want is to drag you down and appease their own feelings of mediocrity and fear... *—U.S. Anderson*

Our negative thoughts are like black wings covering the sun. When we think too many of them, we find ourself living in a world of darkness and gloom... *—Elinor MacDonald*

A cynic is not merely one who reads bitter lessons from the past; he is one who is prematurely disappointed in the future... *—Sydney J. Harris*

When it is dark enough you can see the stars...
—Charles A. Beard

The world is moving so fast these days that the man who says it can't be done is generally interrupted by someone doing it... *—Harry E. Fosdick*

When the outlook is steeped in pessimism, I remind myself, "Two and two still make four, and you can't keep mankind down for long."... *—Bernard M. Baruch*

A pessimist sees only the dark side of the clouds, and mopes; a philosopher sees both sides and shrugs; an optimist doesn't see the clouds at all—he's walking on them... *—D.O. Flynn*

There is no sadder sight than a young pessimist...
—Mark Twain

Possessions

Possessions are generally diminished by possession...
—Friedrich W. Nietzsche

Trying to satisfy one's desires with possessions is like putting out a fire with straw... *—Confucius*

Some day people will learn that material things do not bring happiness... *—Charles P. Steinmetz*

No possession is gratifying without a companion to share it...
—Seneca

Property has its duties as well as its rights...
—Thomas Drummond

The rich man is not one who is in possession of much, but one who gives much... *—John Chrysostom*

The wise man carries his possessions with him...
—Bias of Priene

It is possible to own too much. A man with one watch knows

what time it is; a man with two watches is never quite sure...
—*Lee Segall*

How is it possible to find real happiness in those things which, by their very nature, must pass away?... —*James Allen*

Power

If you make power and fame your goal, even if you attain them, you will find that they don't bring you what you thought they would—it's an empty experience...
—*Dean Ornish*

Power will intoxicate the best hearts, as wine the strongest heads. No man is wise enough, nor good enough to be trusted with unlimited power... —*Charles C. Colton*

Don't fight forces. Use them... —*Buckminster Fuller*

Authority has always attracted the lowest elements of the human race... —*P.J. O'Rourke*

Authority without wisdom is like a heavy axe without an edge, fitter to bruise than polish... —*Anne Bradstreet*

The lust for power, for dominating others, inflames the heart more than any other passion... —*Tacitus*

You only have power over people as long as you don't take everything from them. But when you've robbed a man of everything, he's no longer in your power–he's free again...
—*Alexander Solzhenitsyn*

Power is much more easily manifested in destroying than in creating... —*William Wordsworth*

Power without wisdom falls of its own weight... —*Horace*

Patience and gentleness is power... —*Leigh Hunt*

The measure of man is what he does with power...
—*Pittacus*

I have never been able to conceive how any rational being could propose happiness to himself from the exercise of power over others... —*Thomas Jefferson*

To know the pains of power, we must go to those who have it; to know its pleasures, we must go to those who are seeking it: the pains of power are real, its pleasures imaginary...
—*Charles C. Colton*

Power may be justly compared to a great river; while kept within its bounds it is both beautiful and useful; but when it overflows its banks, it is too impetuous to be stemmed; it bears down all before it, and brings destruction and desolation wherever it comes... —*Andrew Hamilton*

Power is of two kinds. One is obtained by the fear of punishment and the other by the art of love. Power based on love is a thousand times more effective and permanent than the one derived from fear of punishment... —*Plutarch*

He is most powerful who has power over himself...—*Seneca*

Power flows to the man who knows how... —*Elbert Hubbard*

Power always sincerely, conscientiously, believes itself right...Power must never be trusted... —*John Adams*

Unlimited power is apt to corrupt the minds of those who possess it... —*William Penn*

Real power has fullness and variety. It is not narrow like lightning, but broad like light... —*Roswell D. Hitchcock*

The heart declines when power mounts to the head...
—*Henry Hurwitz*

Power is strength and the ability to see yourself through your own eyes and not through the eyes of another. It is being able to place a circle of power at your own feet and not take power from someone else's circle... —*Agnes Whistling Elk*

Prayer

Many times the words of our prayer are in conflict with the real desires of our heart. We pray for one thing when really we want something else... —*Charles L. Allen*

God hears no more than the heart speaks; and if the heart be dumb, God will certainly be deaf... —*Thomas B. Brooks*

There are moments when, whatever be the attitude of the body, the soul is on its knees... —*Victor Hugo*

Do our prayers come true? The answer lies in the way we pray. Let's pray in a way that our prayers are true...
—*Ainsky Meares*

The man who prays longest and loudest...is either trying to convince others or he is trying to convince himself...
—*Fred Van Amburgh*

Prayer is the spirit speaking truth to Truth...—*Philip Bailey*

No cry that goes up from the depths of a sincere heart goes up in vain, and if your prayer is fashioned aright, it will be answered by the god in your own heart... —*Paul Brunton*

Nothing is too small a subject for prayer, because nothing is too small to be the subject of God's care...
—*Henry T. Hamblin*

God is not a cosmic bell–boy for whom we can press a button to get things... —*Harry E. Fosdick*

Pray as if it all depends on God, but work as if it all depends upon you... —*George W. Carver*

The simple heart that freely asks in love, obtains...
—*John G. Whittier*

In prayer it is better to have a heart without words than words without a heart... —*John Bunyan*

We, ignorant of ourselves, beg often our own harms, which the wise powers deny us for our good...
—*William Shakespeare*

Prayer is exhaling the spirit of man and inhaling the spirit of God... —*Edwin Keith*

Prayer is like the turning–on of an electric switch. It does not create the current; it simply provides a channel through which the electric current may flow... —*Max Handel*

I have been driven many times to my knees by the overwhelming conviction that I had nowhere to go...
—*Abraham Lincoln*

Prayer is not flight; prayer is power. Prayer does not deliver a man from some terrible situation; prayer enables a man to face and to master a situation... —*William Barkley*

Prayer! I couldn't live without it; I would have died a thousand times if it had not been for my chance to talk it over with God, and gain strength in it from Him... —*Dale Evans Rogers*

So many times we pray for gifts and favors when we should be praying for the strength to work and the patience to wait...
—*Fred Van Amburgh*

If you would have God hear you when you pray, you must hear Him when he speaks... —*Thomas Brooks*

There is no prayer so blessed as the prayer which asks for nothing... —*Oswald J. Simon*

The fewer the words the better prayer... —*Martin Luther*

Prayers should be the key of the day and the lock of the night... —*English proverb*

We often want one thing and pray for another, not telling the truth even to the gods... —*Seneca*

Every thought of God is prayer... —*Rahel L. Varnhagen*

Prayer is the most perfect and most divine action that a rational soul is capable of. It is of all other actions and duties the most indispensably necessary... —*F. Augustine Baker*

He prays best who does not know that he is praying... —*St. Anthony*

We are always telling God what he can do for us, but to many of us it rarely occurs to ask God what we can do for Him... —*John Powell*

True prayer is not begging or beseeching, it is right knowing. It is not a matter of trying to make something happen, but of becoming aware of that which already is. It is not a time to say "Please" but to say "Thank you."... —*Elinor MacDonald*

We cannot approach prayer as we do everything else in our push–button, instant society. There are no prayer pills... —*Janie Gustafson*

Prayer is conversation with God... —*Josippon*

Prayer is the contemplation of the facts of life from the highest point of view... —*Ralph W. Emerson*

Pride

Proud people breed sorrows for themselves...—*Emily Brontë*

Pride is the mask of one's own faults... —*Hebrew saying*

We are rarely proud when we are alone... —*Voltaire*

The highest and most lofty trees have the most reason to dread the thunder... —*Charles Rollin*

A proud man is always hard to be pleased, because he hath too great expectations from others... —*Richard Baxter*

Whosoever shall exalt himself shall be abased; and he that shall humble himself shall be exalted... —*Jesus*

Principle

Principles are like seeds; they are little things which do much good, if the mind that receives them has the right attitudes... —*Seneca*

If the principle is right, the details will take care of themselves... —*Napoleon Bonaparte*

Back of every noble life there are principles which have fashioned it... —*George H. Lorimer*

Where true principles lack, the results are imperfect... —*Henry Madathanas*

Rely on principles... —*Epictetus*

It is easier to produce ten volumes of philosophical writings than to put one principle into practice... —*Leo Tolstoy*

A new principle is an inexhaustible source of new ideas... —*Luc de Clapiers Vauvenargues*

The moment you use a principle, it will work for you whether it is a principle of mathematics or of the mind... —*Sue Sikking*

Principles are like a seed in the ground, they must continually be visited with heavenly influences or else your life will be a barren field... —*Thomas Traherne*

No single principle can answer all of life's complexities... —*Felix Frankfurter*

Principles don't die. They aren't here one day and gone the next. They can't be destroyed by fire, earthquake or theft.

Principles are deep, fundamental truths, classic truths...
—Stephen R. Covey

Problems

Behind every dark happening, behind every difficulty, there is a hidden blessing... *—White Eagle*

You are yourself your biggest problem. You cannot hand it over to anyone else, be he savior or master, and escape from it, except in delusive imagination or in erroneous belief...
—Paul Brunton

Every problem contains within itself the seeds of its own solution... *—Stanley Arnold*

When everything seems to be going against the wind, remember that the airplane takes off against the wind, not with it... *—Henry Ford*

Suicide is no release from one's problems...All your problems and troubles are in your thinking; so you can see that by losing your body you can't lose your problems, for they are not physical... *—James B. Schafer*

Don't fight your problem. Know that there is a solution...
—Joseph Murphy

Whatever your problem, no matter how difficult, you can release spiritual power sufficient to solve your problem. The secret is–pray and believe... *—Norman V. Peale*

All of your problems and difficulties are the instruction of life, pointing out to you where you are wrong, where you are lacking in wisdom and understanding, where you need to change so that you can open yourself to a greater degree of good than you have yet experienced...
—Elinor MacDonald

Grapple with each new difficulty as it comes up. Wrestle with it till you down it, if it takes until the break of day. Get on top of every difficulty that comes your way. Otherwise, it will get on top of you... —*Archer Brown*

There are two ways of meeting difficulties: you alter the difficulties, or you alter yourself to meet them... —*Phyllis Bottome*

Problems cannot be solved with words, but only through experience... —*Alice Miller*

To every disadvantage there is a corresponding advantage... —*Clement Stone*

There is no such thing as a problem without a gift for you in its hands. You seek problems because you need their gifts... —*Richard Bach*

When life gives you lemons, make lemonade...—*Esco Brown*

Helping others is the best way to rid yourself of your own troubles... —*Edgar Cayce*

To walk against adversity, to bring forth the inner strength, to cope with the problems of life, to walk against the wind of life and push against it makes you breath hard and gives you strength... —*Hilda Charlton*

Whenever a problem appears in our experience, it is because we are strong enough to meet it successfully and overcome it. It is not there to punish us... —*Elinor MacDonald*

Prosperity

Prosperity is only an instrument to be used, not a deity to be worshipped... —*Calvin Coolidge*

We are corrupted by prosperity... —*Tacitus*

Prosperity destroys fools and endangers the wise... —*Henry Bohn*

We become wiser in the midst of adversity; it is prosperity

that takes away righteousness... —*Seneca*

Prosperity is a great teacher; adversity is a greater...
—*William Hazlitt*

Nothing is harder to direct than a man in prosperity; nothing more easily managed than one in adversity... —*Plutarch*

This is the law of prosperity: When apparent adversity comes, be not cast down by it, but make the best of it, and always look forward for better things, for conditions more prosperous...
—*Ralph W. Trine*

Purpose

Learn to get in touch with silence within yourself and know that everything in this life has a purpose...
—*Elisabeth Kubler–Ross*

A man without a purpose is like a ship without a rudder...Have a purpose in life, and having it, throw into your work such strength of mind and muscle as God has given you...
—*Thomas Carlyle*

The great and glorious masterpiece of man is to know how to live to purpose... —*Michel Montaigne*

Purpose is what gives life meaning... —*Charles Parkhurst*

Relationship

A relationship is like a garden. If it is to thrive it must be watered regularly. Special care must be given, taking into accout the seasons as well as any unpredictable weather. New seeds must be sown and weeds must be pulled...
—*John Gray*

Two persons who love each other are in a place more holy than the interior of a church... —*William L. Phelps*

The essential ingredients for relationship are affection and commitment... —*Robert A. Johnson*

It is easier to live through someone else than to become complete yourself... —*Betty Friedan*

Life is a series of relationships—being together and separating... —*Joann Kelley Smith*

Marriage is a box to put your love in. It can hold it safe and warm forever, the door closed against all evil. Or it can be a cage. The box is of your own making... —*Mary Williams*

In all our struggles with relationships, we learn there is a point where we release others to a pattern of their own making... —*Carol W. Parrish–Harra*

No relationship can provide everything needed for the complete experience of being yourself... —*David Viscott*

Sometimes dignity in a marriage can best be preserved when the partners separate before all love dies—in order to work on their individual problems and in order not to hurt each other any more than they already have... —*Sara Kay Cohen*

The false promise is that another person giving you love will solve your problems, make you happy, give you security you desire, make you feel good about yourself...

—*Jordan & Margaret Paul*

The purpose of a relationship is not for two incomplete people to become one, but rather for two complete people to join together for the greater glory of God...

—*Marianne Williamson*

Chains do not hold a marriage together. It is threads, hundreds of tiny threads which sew people together through the years...

—*Simone Signoret*

I believe that we should wise up and recognize that a marriage is a small business and that married couples are business partners... —*David Hopkinson*

Love does not consist in gazing at each other, but in looking outward in the same direction... —*Antoine de Saint-Exupery*

There is no relationship that is more important than your relationship with yourself—it affects all others and everything that you do in life... —*Sharon Garell*

The highest love a person can have for you is to wish for you to evolve into the best person you can be. No one owns you, no matter what your relationship... —*David Viscott*

Don't attempt to perpetuate a relationship by contract...Try to avoid any situation in which you or anyone else is obligated...You wouldn't get good value when the individual no longer wants to be involved... —*Harry Browne*

Powerful relationships arise when two centered individuals commit themselves to unconditionally love one another and to support each other's growth toward full potential...
—*Thomas Crum*

The most empowering relationships are those in which each partner lifts the other to a higher possession of their own being... —*Teilhard de Chardin*

No other person can bring us happiness if she or he does not possess it herself or himself. The romantic urge to seek in a second individual that which neither of the two has, can never find successful fulfillment... —*Paul Brunton*

Relationships are like a dance, with visible energy racing back and forth between the partners... —*Colette Dowling*

Relationships are only as alive as the people engaging in them... —*Donald B. Ardell*

I do my thing, and you do your thing. I am not in this world to live up to your expectations, and you are not in this world to live up to mine. You are you and I am I. If by chance we find each other, it's beautiful. If not, it can't be helped...
—Fritz Perls

Religion

The poverty of all religions has been their inability to make God real to their devotees... *—Julian P. Johnson*

For true worship, only God and the human soul are necessary. It does not depend upon times, or seasons, or occasions. Anywhere and at any time God and man in the bush may meet...
—Ralph W. Trine

Forms are but symbols; we should never rest in them, but make them the stepping stones to the good to which they point... *—Nathaniel Emmons*

Any religion in which a man is good—and unbigoted—is a good religion for him and should be held in esteem...
—Caroline Duerr

What we need in religion is not new light, but new sight, not new paths, but new strength to walk in the old ones...
—Tryon Edwards

True religion and virtue give a cheerful and happy turn to the mind... *—Joseph Addison*

Your religion is where your love is... *—Henry D. Thoreau*

The spiritual is not religious. A religion is dogma, a set of beliefs about the spiritual and a set of practices which rise out of those beliefs... *—Rachel N. Remen*

Religion is nothing else but love of God and man...
—William Penn

Religion is regarded by the common people as true, by the wise as false, and by the rulers as useful... —*Seneca*

Unselfishness is the only real religion... —*Israel Zangwill*

True religion needs neither arms nor fingers for its use; it is all spirit and heart... —*Moses Mendelssohn*

Science without religion is lame, religion without science is blind... —*Albert Einstein*

Religion holds a man back from the path, prevents his stepping forward, for various very plain reasons. First, it makes the vital mistake of distinguishing between good and evil...

—*Mabel Collins*

Temples are not to be built for Him with stones piled on high; God is to be concentrated in the breast of each...

—*Seneca*

Saints

Saints are not saints by chance, nor by choice, but by necessity—because there is a hunger in their souls which cannot be satisfied by anything less than the divine...

—*Nancy Pope Mayyorya*

Saints are simply men and women who have fulfilled their natural obligation, which is to approach God...

—*Evelyn Waugh*

Whoever fights ceaselessly against his own selfishness and strives to supplant it with all–embracing love is a saint, whether he live in a cottage or in the midst of riches and influence; or whether he preaches or remains obscure...

—*James Allen*

All good men are saints.. —*Francois Fenelon*

The creed of the saint is to make the most of life, and to make the best of it... —*Edwin H. Chapin*

The saints of God are sealed inwardly with faith, but outwardly with good works... —*John Boys*

The saints of God are known by three signs: their thought is of God, their dwelling is with God, and their business is in God... —*Attar*

Search/Look Within

Nothing gives rest but the sincere search for truth...
—*Blaise Pascal*

You search of God, and seek to find Him here. Or you seek to find Him there. Why need you look in the corners of the room when He entirely fills the room... —*Ormond McGill*

If you can find the God inside yourself, you can find the God inside everybody... —*Stephen Levine*

Science cannot solve the ultimate mystery of Nature. And it is because in the last analysis we ourselves are part of the mystery we are trying to solve... —*Max Planck*

You never know yourself till you know more than your body...
—*Thomas Traherne*

When one is a stranger to oneself then one is estranged from others too... —*Anne Morrow Lindbergh*

What lies behind us and what lies before us are tiny matters compared to what lies within us... —*Oliver W. Holmes*

Until we lose ourselves there is no hope of finding ourselves...
—*Henry Miller*

When a man's fight begins within himself, he is worth something... —*Robert Browning*

Look at your own life. Has it become overly complex? Have you found yourself burdened by too many possessions or responsibilities? Take a deep breath and ask yourself: "What steps can I take to reduce the clutter so that I may live simply and joyously?"... —*Douglas Bloch*

The important thing is not to stop questioning...
—*Albert Einstein*

In each of us there is a king. Speak to him and he will come forth... —*Danish proverb*

Seek ye first the kingdom of God, and his righteousness, and all things will be added unto you... —*Jesus*

The height of all philosophy is to know thyself; and the end of this knowledge is to know God... —*Francis Quarles*

If we know that God is forever right where we are, we shall not be reaching out in every direction for Him...
—*Ernest Holmes*

For thirty years I went in search of God, and when at the end of that time I opened my eyes, I discovered that it was he who had been looking for me... —*Bayezid Bistami*

I want to know how God created this world. I am not interested in this or that phenomenon. I want to know His thoughts, the rest are details... —*Albert Einstein*

Secreted and hidden in the heart of the world and in the heart of man is the light which can illuminate all life, the future and the past. Shall we not search for it?...
—*Mabel Collins*

We seek satisfaction in the baubles of the world, yet we discover no satisfaction at all, but only disappointment and despair. Finding no solace anywhere, we at last turn to reality where alone true satisfaction may be found...
—*Henry T. Hamblin*

Self–Esteem

He who undervalues himself is justly undervalued by others...
—William Hazlitt

The lower our self–esteem, the more we're attracted to our opposite, and the higher our self–esteem, the more we are attracted to another like ourselves... *—Marilyn vos Savant*

Self–confidence is a good thing to develop, after you are sure you have something to be confident about...
—Fred Van Amburgh

I have an everyday religion that works for me. Love yourself first and everything else falls into place... *—Lucille Ball*

It is difficult to make a man miserable while he feels he is worthy of himself and claims kindred to the great God who made him... *—Abraham Lincoln*

He that respects himself is safe from others; he wears a coat of mail that none can pierce... *—Henry W. Longfellow*

If you don't like yourself, you can't be happy...
—Dennis Wholey

It is a psychological fact that man always conforms to the image he holds of himself. Change his image and you change his actions, his reactions, his environment, his world...
—Jack Holland

Lack of confidence is not the result of difficulty; the difficulty comes from lack of confidence... *—Seneca*

Above all things, revere yourself... *—Pythagoras*

Believe in yourself; feel that you are able to dominate your surroundings. Resolve that you will be master and not the slave of circumstances... *—Orison S. Marden*

If I am not for myself, who will be for me?... *—Hillel*

A man cannot be comfortable without his own approval...
—*Mark Twain*

How can we send the highest love to others if we do not have it for ourselves?... —*Prentice Mulford*

Selfishness

As a man goes down in self, he goes up in God...
—*George B. Cheever*

The hardest victory is the victory over self... —*Aristotle*

Look in the mirror every day, for if scars of selfishness or pride are in the heart, they will grow into lines on the face. Watch closely... —*Etu Inagaki Sugimoto*

Selfishness is the great enemy of peace. Selfishness walks by itself and no one walks with it... —*Blackfeather*

No man is more cheated than the selfish man...
—*Henry W. Beecher*

The reason why lovers and their mistresses never tire of being together is that they are always talking of themselves...
—*Francois La Rochefoucauld*

The disease we all have and that we have to fight against all our lives is, of course, the disease of self...
—*Sherwood Anderson*

The selfish man suffers more from his selfishness than he from whom that selfishness withholds some important benefit... —*Ralph W. Emerson*

Half the harm that is done in the world is due to people who want to feel important... —*T.S. Eliot*

A man is called selfish, not for pursuing his own good, but for neglecting his neighbor's... —*Richard Whatly*

Self–Realization

We know what we are, but know not what we may be...
—*William Shakespeare*

There's only one corner of the universe you can be certain of improving: that's your own self... —*Aldous Huxley*

Before we can change others, we must first change ourselves. This is a case of where charity really does begin at home, and by beginning to cleanse ourselves of those fears and dreads, uncertainties, wishful thinking, might be's and maybe's, we come to a complete acceptance of spiritual realization... —*Ronald Beesley*

What stands between a man and his self–realization is metaphysical ignorance; and the ultimate goal...is the elimination of that ignorance... —*Amaury de Reincourt*

Self–Reliance

Pray to God but continue to row the boat to shore...
—*Russian proverb*

He who is being carried does not realize how far the next town is... —*African proverb*

The only person I control in the entire world is me...
—*Ralph Stayer*

Everyone can raise himself, but only by his own actions...
—*Nahman Bratzlav*

You can depend upon no man, upon no friend, but on him who depends upon himself. Only he who acts beneficially towards himself will act so towards others...
—*John K. Lavater*

They can conquer who believe they can... —*Virgil*

Help thyself, and God will be there... —*George Herbert*

The strongest man in the world is he who stands most alone... —*Henrik Ibsen*

God helps those who help themselves...—*Benjamin Franklin*

Heaven never helps the man who will not act... —*Sophocles*

No bird soars too high, if he soars with his own wings... —*William Blake*

Self–reverence, self–knowledge, self–control, these three alone lead to sovereign power... —*Alfred L. Tennyson*

Every tub must stand on its own bottom... —*Charles Macklin*

Self–reliance is only a part of the picture. When we carry it to the extreme, we cut ourselves off from others and from the nourishment we need from them... —*Melvyn Kinder*

The strength whereby God saves is the strength that is our own... —*Israel Zangwill*

Self–confidence without self–reliance is as useless as a cooking recipe without food. Self–confidence sees the possibilities of the individual; self–reliance realizes them. Self–confidence sees the angel in the unhewn block of marble; self–reliance carves it out for himself... —*William G. Jordan*

Service

Great opportunities to help others seldom come, but small ones surround us daily... —*Sally Koch*

When a blind man carries a lame man, both are able to go forward... —*Swedish proverb*

It is true that if we look after others, God will look after us—and do a lot better job of it than we can... —*Arthur E. Yensen*

Desire to sow no seed for your own harvesting; desire only to sow that seed, the fruit of which shall feed the world. You are a part of the world; in giving it food you feed yourself...

—Mabel Collins

The way you begin to change the world is through service...

—Martin L. King, Jr.

Joy can be real only if people look upon their life as a service, and have a definite object in life outside themselves and their personal happiness... *—Leo Tolstoy*

Service of God consists in what we do to our neighbor...

—Leo Baeck

You can't live a perfect day without doing something for someone who will never be able to repay you...

—John Wooden

The great happiness in life is not to donate but to serve...

—Louis Brandeis

Through our willingness to help others we can learn to be happy rather than depressed... *—Gerald Jampolsky*

It is not what we see and touch or that which others do for us which makes us happy; it is that which we think and feel and do, first for the other fellow and then for ourselves...

—Helen Keller

SERVICE. A beautiful word fallen upon bad days...

—Claude McKay

Do all the good you can, by all the means you can, in all the ways you can, in all the places you can, all the times you can, to all the people you can, as long as you can...*—John Wesley*

The most acceptable service of God is doing good to man...

—Benjamin Franklin

We need to be needed. Service to others can give us a new purpose in life... *—Abbe Pierre*

They serve God well, who serve his creations...
—*Caroline Norton*

Silence

What is it that stands higher than words? Action. What is it that stands higher than action? Silence... —*Francis of Assisi*

True silence really means going deep within yourself to that place where nothing is happening, where you transcend time and space. You go into a brand new dimension of nothingness. That's where all the power is. That's your real home. That's where you really belong, in deep silence where there is no good or bad, no one trying to achieve anything. Just being, pure being...Silence is the ultimate reality... —*Robert Adams*

There is silence, the child of love, which expresses everything, and proclaims more loudly than the tongue is able to do... —*Vittorio Alfieri*

The truest communication with God is absolute, total silence; there is not a single word in existence that can convey this communication... —*Bernadette Roberts*

Silence is the element in which great things fashion themselves together... —*Thomas Carlyle*

Silence is the language God speaks, and everything else is a bad translation... —*Thomas Keating*

It is easier to be altogether silent than not to exceed in words... —*Thomas à Kempis*

I like the silent church, before the service begins, better than preaching... —*Ralph W. Emerson*

There is no explanation quite so effective as silence...
—*Alfred A. Montapert*

He can never speak well who knows not how to hold his peace... —*Plutarch*

We need a reason to speak, but none to keep silent...
—*Pierre Nicole*

There are silent depths in the ocean which storms that lash the surface into fury never reach... —*Orison S. Marden*

Life teaches us silently while men utter their instruction in loud voices... —*Paul Brunton*

Silence is more eloquent than words... —*Thomas Carlyle*

Silence is wisdom's best reply... —*Euripides*

The highest thoughts are those least dependent on language... —*John Ruskin*

The ancient sentence said, "Let us be silent for so are the gods." Silence is a solvent that destroys personality, and gives us leave to be great and universal... —*Ralph W. Emerson*

Silence is a healing for all ailments... —*Babylonian Talmud*

Prayer begins by talking to God, but it ends by listening to Him. In the face of Absolute Truth, silence is the soul's language... —*Fulton J. Sheen*

Simplicity

The ability to simplify means to eliminate the unnecessary so that the necessary may speak... —*Hans Hofmann*

Purity and simplicity are the two wings with which man soars above the earth and all temporary nature...
—*Thomas à Kempis*

It does not matter whether one paints a picture, writes a poem, or carves a statue—simplicity is the mark of a master hand... —*Elsie De Wolfe*

Nothing is better than simplicity... —*Walt Whitman*

A simple life is its own reward... —*George Santayana*

Very little is needed to make a happy life... —*Ptolemy*

Life is not complex. We are complex. Life is simple and the simple thing is the right thing... —*Oscar Wilde*

Simple style is like white light. It is complex but its complexity is not obvious... —*Anatole France*

Less is more... —*Robert Browning*

Simplicity, of all things, is the hardest to be copied... —*Richard Steele*

The more complicated life becomes, the more people are attracted to simple solutions... —*James Reston*

The art of art, the glory of expression and the sunshine of the light of letters, is simplicity... —*Walt Whitman*

Simplicity is the peak of civilization... —*Jessie Sampter*

The higher the truth, the simpler it is... —*Abraham Kook*

Blessed are the simple, for they shall have much peace... —*Thomas à Kempis*

I am bound to praise the simple life, because I have lived it and found it good... —*John Burroughs*

The only simplicity that matters is the simplicity of the heart... —*G.K. Chesterton*

Smile

A smile is ever the most bright and beautiful with a tear upon it... —*Walter S. Landor*

We can not open our hearts to give out cheer without more cheer rushing in to takes its place... —*Alice H. Rice*

Some people are too tired to give you a smile. Give them one of yours, as no one needs a smile so much as one who has none to give... —*Frank I. Fletcher*

Smiles are like pebbles cast into the water. The ripples spread and spread... *—Fred Van Amburgh*

The cheerful live longest in years and afterwards in our regards. Cheerfulness is the offshoot of goodness...
—Christian Bovee

Every time a man smiles, and much more when he laughs, it adds something to his fragment of life... *—Laurence Sterne*

When we learn to smile at life, we shall find that the problems we encounter dissolve... *—Donald Curtis*

Those who bring sunshine into the lives of others cannot keep it from themselves... *—James M. Barrie*

I have often been asked what I thought was the secret of Buddha's smile. It is–it can only be–that he smiled at himself for searching all those years for what he already possessed...
—Paul Brunton

If you force yourself to smile, you'll end up laughing. You will be cheerful because you smile... *—Kenneth Goode*

If you're not using your smile, you're like a man with a million dollars in the bank and no checkbook... *—Les Giblin*

Cheerfulness is the great lubricant of the wheels of life. It lightens labor, diminishes difficulties, and mitigates misfortunes... *—Alfred A. Montapert*

Of cheerfulness...the more it is spent, the more of it remains...
—Ralph W. Emerson

In speaking of others always be calm and cheerful...
—Teresa of Avila

The mind that is cheerful will have no concern for the future, and will meet the bitterness of life with a smile...
—Horace

A fool raises his voice when he laughs, but a wise man smiles quietly... —*Ben Sirach*

A cheerful friend is like a sunny day, which sheds its brightness on all around... —*John Lubbock*

Solitude

You find in solitude only what you take to it...
—*Juan R. Jimenez*

A solitude is an audience–chamber with God...
—*Walter S. Landor*

Solitude, if rightly used, becomes not only a privilege but a necessity. Only a superficial soul fears to fraternize with itself... —*Alice H. Rice*

Very few things keep their charm in solitude; and if the solitude is absolute and complete, everything turns irretrievably to ashes... —*Fernando Savater*

Inside myself is a place, where I live all alone, and that's where you renew your springs that never dry up...
—*Pearl S. Buck*

Solitude is fine when you are at peace with yourself and have something definite to do... —*Johann W. Goethe*

Conversation enriches the understanding, but solitude is the school of genius... —*Edward Gibbon*

No man will unfold the capacities of his own intellect who does not at least checker his life with solitude...
—*Thomas De Quincey*

Only in complete loneliness do we learn the true meaning of the words: know thyself! For only then do we stand before our own true selves... —*Hans–Ulrich Rieker*

Inspiration makes solitude anywhere... —*Ralph W. Emerson*

Solitude is the highest stage. Only in solitude can man attain...union with the eternal God... —*Nahman Bratzlav*

Solitude gives birth to the original in us... —*Thomas Mann*

Solitary trees, if they grow at all, grow strong...
—*Winston Churchill*

Man cannot survive without air, water and sleep. Next in importance comes food. And close on its heels, solitude...
—*Thomas Szasz*

To live a spiritual life we must first find the courage to enter into the desert of loneliness and change it by gentle and persistent efforts into a garden of solitude...
—*Henry J. Nouwen*

Even in paradise, it is good to be alone... —*Jewish proverb*

A wise man is never less alone than when he is alone...
—*Jonathan Swift*

Settle yourself in solitude, and you will come upon God in yourself... —*Teresa of Avila*

A certain degree of solitude seems necessary to the full growth and spread of the highest mind...
—*Friedrich von Novalis*

It is well to be alone. It fertilizes the creative impulse...
—*Max Nordau*

Rest is more perfect than movement, and for the sake of rest the individual things are moved... —*Marsilio Ficino*

Men fear silence as they fear solitude, because both give them a glimpse of the terror of life's nothingness...
—*Andre Maurois*

Solitude is the nurse of enthusiasm, and enthusiasm is the parent of genius... —*Isaac D'Israeli*

It is easy in the world to live after the world's opinion; it is easy in solitude to live after your own; but the great man is he who, in the midst of a crowd, keeps with perfect sweetness the independence of solitude... *—Ralph W. Emerson*

They are never alone that are accompanied with noble thoughts... *—Philip Sidney*

You cannot build a character in a solitude; you need a formed character to stand a solitude... *—Austin O'Malley*

It would do the world good if every man in it would compel himself occasionally to be absolutely alone. Most of the world's progress has come out of such loneliness... *—Bruce Barton*

Speech

Once a word has been allowed to escape, it cannot be recalled... *—Horace*

If you stop talking and stop thinking, there will be nothing you do not understand... *—Paul Twitchell*

When the mouth stumbles, it is worse than the foot... *—West African proverb*

Speech is a mirror of the soul; as a man speaks, so he is... *—Publilius Syrus*

We cannot talk about atoms in ordinary language... *—Werner Heisenberg*

One of the things that keep us at a distance from perfection is, without doubt, our tongue... *—Francis de Sales*

Nature has given us two ears, two eyes, and but one tongue, to the end that we should hear and see more than we speak... *—Epictetus*

The less you speak the less you err... *—Solomon Ibn Gabirol*

The less men think, the more they talk...
—*Charles Montesquieu*

It is easier to talk than to hold one's tongue...
—*Greek proverb*

Be in no hurry to speak... —*Old Testament*

Talkative people listen to no one, for they are ever speaking. And the first evil surrounding those who do not know the meaning of silence is that they hear nothing... —*Epictetus*

Speech is the small change of silence... —*George Meredith*

They always talk who never think... —*Matthew Prior*

He who speaks becomes silent before the Divine Essence...
—*Jili*

Do not trust all who talk smoothly. Listen much and speak little... —*Robert Benson*

Talk that does not end in any kind of action is better suppressed altogether... —*Thomas Carlyle*

Spirituality

The man who has no inner life is a slave of his surroundings, as the barometer is the obedient servant of the air...
—*Henri F. Amiel*

Spirituality does not "separate" you from the world; it allows you to connect with All There Is, and that includes your life here... —*Iris Belhayes*

Spirituality is like a bird; if you hold on to it tightly, it chokes, and if you hold it loosely, it escape... —*Israel Lipkin*

Zen does not confuse spirituality with thinking about God while one is peeling potatoes. Zen spirituality is just to peel the potatoes... —*Alan Watts*

We are not human beings having a spiritual experience. We are spiritual beings having a human experience...

—Teilhard de Chardin

Spirit is strong but flesh is weak, so weak sometimes it even overpowers the strong spirit 'which knows all truth'...

—H.P. Blavatsky

Your spirit is everything; your body is a garment that rots, and nothing more... *—Allan Kardec*

Success

If you would have a successful life, less and less try to make things happen and more and more just let things happen...

—Ormond McGill

Do your job naturally because you like it and success will take care of itself... *—Norman V. Peale*

Success is how high you bounce when you hit bottom...

—George Patton

Success is more dangerous than failure. The ripples break over a wider coastline... *—Graham Greene*

If you hit every time, the target is too near or too big...

—Tom Hirshfield

Success makes life easier. It doesn't make living easier...

—Bruce Springsteen

Success is going from one failure to the next without a loss of enthusiasm... *—Winston Churchill*

Success seems to be largely a matter of hanging on after others have let go... *—William Feather*

Many people dream of success. To me, success can only be achieved through repeated failure and introspection. In fact, success represents the one percent of your work which results only from the ninety–nine percent that is called failure...

—Soichiro Honda

Always bear in mind that your own resolution to success is more important than any other one thing...

—Abraham Lincoln

Successful people are not gifted; they just work hard—then succeed on purpose... *—G.K. Neilson*

Success is a series of right thoughts put into action...

—Fred Van Amburgh

Try not to become a man of success. Rather become a man of value... *—Albert Einstein*

The secret of all success is commitment. No one has ever received, gained, or accomplished anything in life without first being deeply committed to it... *—Alan Cohen*

A wise man will make more opportunities than he finds...

—Francis Bacon

The hopeful man sees success where others see failure, sunshine where others see shadows and storm...

—Orison S. Marden

The secret of success is constancy of purpose...

—Benjamin Disraeli

If you think you can do something, you have a much better chance for success than if you wish you could...

—Tom Kubistant

The surest way to miss success is to miss the opportunity...

—Philarete Charles

Never stop being creative. The more you practice, the more creative you become. Creativity spells success...

—Alden James

I measure success by how well I sleep at night. If I am at peace with my God and myself, I fall asleep easily. If sleep comes hard, then I know the day has been a perfect failure...
—*Rod McKuen*

There are three primary principles essential to the success of any venture. They are simple, but important: 1. Determine your objectives. 2. Analyze the obstacles in your way. 3. Learn how to overcome your obstacles... —*Dick Carlson*

There are no secrets to success. It's the result of preparation, hard work, learning from failure... —*Colin L. Powell*

Personal success is never static. It usually comes in small steps leading to other small steps that lead to broader achievement...
—*Wess Roberts*

The key to success is to feel your "work" is "play."...
—*Michael Korda*

Self–trust is the first secret of success... —*Ralph W. Emerson*

Great successes never come without risks...
—*Flavius Josephus*

We can do anything we want to do if we stick with it long enough... —*Helen Keller*

Suffering

The hardships of life are not sent by an unkind destiny to crush, but to challenge... —*Sam E. Roberts*

To become the spectator of one's own life is to escape the suffering of life... —*Oscar Wilde*

Sorrow is a gentle teacher, and reveals many things that would be hard to understand... —*Anna Brown Lindsay*

Life is truly known only to those who suffer, lose, endure adversity and stumble from defeat to defeat...
—*Ryszard Kapuscinski*

Sorrow makes us all children again, destroys all differences of intellect. The wisest knows nothing... —*Ralph W. Emerson*

Sorrow and suffering give opportunities for growth. Disappointment opens doors to wider fields...
—*Elizabeth Gray Vining*

Sorrow washes the eyes with the tears of more perfect understanding... —*Fred Van Amburgh*

Man cannot remake himself without suffering. For he is both the marble and the sculptor... —*Alexis Carrel*

Sorrow is a fruit; God does not allow it to grow on a branch that is too weak to bear it... —*Victor Hugo*

Every tunnel has its end... —*Comte de Saint Germaine*

Love your suffering. Do not resist it, do not flee from it. Give yourself to it. It is only your aversion that hurts, nothing else...
—*Hermann Hesse*

Earth has no sorrow that Heaven cannot heal...
—*Thomas More*

Sorrow, like rain, makes roses and mud...
—*Austin O'Maliey*

The diamond cannot be polished without friction, nor man perfected without trials... —*Confucius*

To realize that one's creation necessitates one's suffering, that suffering is one of the greatest of God's gifts, is almost to reach a mystical solution of the problem of evil...
—*J.W. Sullivan*

Tears are the best of God to suffering man... —*John Keble*

God washes the eyes by tears until they behold the invisible land where tears shall come no more... —*Henry W. Beecher*

Surrender

Whosoever shall seek to save his life shall lose it; and whosoever shall lose his life shall find it... —*Jesus*

What prevents us from total surrender is also the cause of our other troubles. It is our selfish will... —*Piero Ferrucci*

The thing we surrender to becomes our power... —*Ernest Holmes*

If you realize what the real problem is—losing yourself, giving yourself to some higher end...you realize that this itself is the ultimate trial... —*Joseph Campbell*

If your mountain will not move, surrender it to God. He will either move it or show you how to turn it into a mine or a monument... —*Robert Schuller*

Yes God! Yes God! Yes, yes and always yes... —*Nicolas de Cusa*

Teacher

First, teach a person to develop to the point of his limitation and then—pfft!–break the limitation... —*Viola Spolin*

The years teach much which the days never know... —*Ralph W. Emerson*

A good teacher must be able to put himself in the place of those who find learning hard... —*Eliphas Levi*

You are your own best teacher... —*Warren Bennis*

You will find something more in the woods than in books. Trees and stones will teach you that which you can never learn from masters... —*St. Bernard*

By learning you will teach; by teaching you will learn... —*Latin aphorism*

Every man I meet is my superior in some way. In that, I learn from him... —*Ralph W. Emerson*

The teaching which is written on paper is not the true teaching. Written teaching is a kind of food for the brain...

—*Shunryn Suzuki*

He teaching who gives, and he learns who receives...

—*Ralph W. Emerson*

You teach best what you most need to learn...

—*Richard Bach*

In the school of life, everything that happens to you is a teaching, and everyone is your teacher. Think of your experiences as coded messages that are saying, "There is something that you have to learn in order to grow and to expand."... —*Douglas Bloch*

Men learn while they teach... —*Seneca*

The art of teaching is the art of assisting discovery...

—*Mark Van Doren*

Nature is the universal teacher. Whatever we cannot learn from the external appearance of Nature, we can learn from her spirit. Both are one... —*Paraceslus*

Thoughts

Nobody can tell you how to think, unless you permit him to do so. Herein lies your greatest glory...and (up to now) one of your greatest sources of trouble... —*Elinor MacDonald*

Creative thinking may simply mean the realization that there is no particular virtue in doing things the way they have always been done... —*Rudolph Flesch*

Time is of no account with great thoughts. They are as fresh today as when they first passed through their authors' minds, ages ago... —*Samuel Smiles*

We know what a person thinks not when he tells us what he thinks, but by his actions... —*Isaac Bashevis Singer*

Everything you think vibrates through your body...
—*Bobbie Probstein*

People who are able to do their own thinking should not allow others to do it for them... —*Elbert Hubbard*

Nothing is good or bad, but thinking makes it so...
—*William Shakespeare*

Change your thoughts and you change your world...
—*Norman V. Peale*

We are all living is a vast ocean of thought. Thoughts are forces...They have form, quality and substance...
—*Ralph W. Trine*

Thought is a mirror: it shows man the ugliness and the beauty within him... —*Moses Ibn Ezra*

How did man get out of the Kingdom of God? How did he lose his place in it? By his negative thinking...
—*Robert A. Russell*

All that is wrong, is wrong as thinking makes it such...
—*Francis Bacon*

Think like a man of action, and act like a man of thought...
—*Henri Bergson*

Man is a plant which bears thoughts, just as a rose tree bears roses and an apple tree bears apples... —*Antoine F. D'Olivet*

Our thought is the key which unlocks the doors of the universe... —*Samuel M. Crothess*

Negative thoughts are the world's most communicable disease... —*Gene E. Clark*

The way we are going to think tomorrow depends largely on what we are thinking today... —*David L. Brown*

Time

He is the best teacher who makes the best use of his time and that of his pupils. For time is all that is given by God in which to do the work of improvement...—*Emma H. Willard*

Time is not a line, but a series of now–points... —*Taisen Deshimaru*

You will never 'find' time for anything. If you want time you must make it... —*Charles Buxton*

When there is a stain, and nothing will remove it—time will take it away... —*William Buck*

We talk about saving time and killing time when actually we can't do either. We have no choice but to spend it at a constant and flowing rate... —*Michael LeBeouf*

Time is chief ingredient in judgement... —*William Feather*

Time is a kindly God... —*Sophocles*

How you spend your time is more important than how you spend your money. Money mistakes can be corrected, but time is gone forever... —*David Norris*

Time is a circus always packing up and moving away... —*Ben Hecht*

We have time enough if we will use it aright... —*Johann W. Goethe*

Time...moves slowly to him whose employment is to watch its flight... —*Samuel Johnson*

Time heals what reason cannot... —*Seneca*

Truth

Truth will always win in a free and open encounter...
—Richard Rorty

The truth is sort of mysterious and sometimes has nothing to do with facts... *—Oliver Sacks*

I believe that in the end the truth will conquer...
—John Wycliffe

If I held Truth in my hand, I should let it go, for the joy of pursuing it is greater than that of finding it...
—William Hamilton

Truth is too simple for us; we do not like those who unmask our illusions... *—Ralph W. Emerson*

In the mountains of truth, you never climb in vain...
—Friedrich W. Nietzsche

Truth is tough. It will not break, like a bubble, at a touch...you may kick it about all day like a football, and it will be round and full at evening... *—Oliver W. Holmes*

If you seek truth, you will not seek to gain a victory by every possible means; and when you have found the truth, you need not fear being defeated... *—Epictetus*

Hardly one in ten thousand will have the strength of mind to ask himself seriously and earnestly, "Is that true?"...
—Arthur Schopenhauer

The truth is more important than facts... *—Frank L. Wright*

We know the truth; not only by reason, but also by the heart...
—Blaise Pascal

You shall know the truth and the truth shall make you free...
—Jesus

Because God lives within you, then truth lives within you...
—*Albert E. Cliffe*

The man who finds a truth lights a torch... —*Robert Ingersoll*

The language of truth is unadorned and simple...
—*Marcellinus Ammianus*

There is an inmost center in all of us where Truth abides in fullness... —*Robert Browning*

Accept the truth: whatever the source...take the pearls from the sea, the gold from the dust, and the roses from amidst the thorns... —*Emmanuel*

The simplest questions are the hardest to answer...
—*Northrop Frye*

The city of truth cannot be built on the swampy ground of skepticism... —*Albert Schweitzer*

To seek for the truth, for the sake of knowing the truth, is one of the noblest objects a man can live for... —*Dean Inge*

He who is not true himself will not see the truth...
—*Paracelsus*

Hard are the ways of truth, and rough to walk...
—*John Milton*

Truth may be stretched, but cannot be broken, and always gets above falsehood, as oil does above water...
—*Miguel de Cervantes*

To love God and love the truth are one and the same...
—*Silvio Pellico*

Truth has no special time of its own. Its hour is now–always...
—*Albert Schweitzer*

War

If it's natural to kill why do men have to go into training to learn how?... *—Joan Baez*

Can anything be more ridiculous than that a man has a right to kill because he dwells on the other side of the water, and because his prince has a quarrel with mine, athough I have none with him... *—Blaise Pascal*

In peace, sons bury their fathers; in wars, fathers bury their sons... *—Herodotus*

Fighting is like champagne. It goes to the heads of cowards as quickly as of heros. Any fool can be brave on a battlefield when it's be brave or else be killed... *—Margaret Mitchell*

War is the child of pride, and pride the daughter of riches... *—Jonathan Swift*

During war we imprison the rights of man... *—Jean Giraudoux*

A "just war" is a contradiction in terms... *—John Quinn*

There is a war going on at the present moment. What does it signify? It signifies that several millions of sleeping people are trying to destroy several millions of other sleeping people. They would not do this, of course, if they were awake.. *—George I. Gurdjieff*

I find war detestable, but even more detestable are those who praise war without participating in it... *—Romain Rolland*

War: first, one hopes to win; then, one expects the enemy to lose; then, one is satisfied that he too is suffering; in the end, one is surprised that everyone has lost... *—Karl Kraus*

Wars are not fought for territory, but for words. Man's deadliest weapon is language. He is as susceptible to being hypnotized by slogans as he is to infectious diseases...

—Arthur Koestler

War is only a cowardly escape from the problems of peace...

—Thomas Mann

The greatest curse that can be entailed on mankind is a state of war... *—Sydney Smith*

Every war is a national misfortune... *—Helmuth von Moltke*

Preparation for war is a constant stimulus to suspicion and ill will... *—James Monroe*

If sunbeams were weapons of war, we would have had solar energy long ago... *—George Porter*

The guns and the bombs, the rockets and the warships, all are symbols of human failure... *—Lyndon B. Johnson*

Men will fight and die without knowing what they are fighting and dying for... *—Douglas MacArthur*

War. There is no solution for it. There is never a conqueror. The winner generates such hatred that he is ultimately defeated... *—Michel Simon*

War is the science of destruction... *—John S. C. Abbot*

Wars are not "acts of God." They are caused by man, by man-made institutions, by the way in which man has organized society. What man has made, man can change...

—Frederick M. Vinson

War is that condition which uses man's best to man's worst...

—Harry E. Fosdick

Wealth

No one has had the courage to memorialize his wealth on his tombstone. A dollar sign would not look good there...
—Corra M. Harris

No man can tell whether he is rich or poor by turning to his ledger. It is the heart that makes a man rich. He is rich according to what he is, not according to what he has...
—Henry W. Beecher

Man's greatest wealth is to live on a little with contented mind; for a little is never lacking... *—Julius Caesar*

Wealth is the diploma of slavery...A great fortune is a great slavery... *—Seneca*

Wealth is like sea–water; the more we drink, the thirstier we become... *—Arthur Schopenhauer*

The only thing wealth does for some people is to make them worry about losing it... *—Comte de Rivarol*

Real wealth is the soul in repose... *—Samuel Hoffenstein*

Without a rich heart, wealth is an ugly beggar...
—Ralph W. Emerson

No wealth in the world can help humanity forward, even in the hands of the most devoted worker in this cause...
—Albert Einstein

Very few men acquire wealth in such a manner as to receive pleasure from it... *—Henry W. Beecher*

One of the main reasons wealth makes people unhappy is that it gives them too much control over what they experience. They try to translate their own fantasies into reality instead of tasting what reality itself has to offer...
—Philip Slater

To be rich is not the end, but only a change of worries...
—*Epicurus*

The best and safest way of getting wealth is to work for it...
—*Queen Elizabeth of Rumania*

Wisdom

The heart of a wise man lies quiet like still water...
—*Cameroonian proverb*

Wisdom never kicks at the iron walls it can't bring down...
—*Olive Schreiner*

Who is a wise man? He who learns from all men...
—*The Talmud*

Wisdom is to see the miraculous in the common...
—*Ralph W. Emerson*

All human wisdom is summed up in two words—wait and hope...
—*Alexandre Dumas*

The art of being wise is the art of knowing what to overlook...
—*William James*

The more I know, the more I realize I don't know...
—*Albert Einstein*

The wise man is never surprised by death: he is always ready to depart...
—*Jean La Fontaine*

Wisdom is like gold ore, mixed with stones and dust...
—*Moses Ibn Ezra*

If we desire wisdom we must seek for it, work for it, and pray for it. We must patiently strive for the wisdom that we desire and then we must pass it out to others who are also seeking wisdom...
—*Amber M. Tuttle*

Pain is the father, and love is the mother, of wisdom...
—*Ludwig Borne*

Cleverness is not wisdom... —*Euripides*

From the errors of others a wise man corrects his own... —*Publilius Syrus*

Wisdom is the child of experience... —*John F. Kennedy*

Is there not one true coin for which all things ought to be exchanged?—and that is wisdom. —*Plato*

A wise man hears one word and understands two... —*Yiddish saying*

Who is wise? He that learns from everybody... —*Benjamin Franklin*

One cannot have wisdom without living life... —*Dorothy McCall*

It is not wise to be wiser than necessary...—*Philippe Quinault*

Knowledge is power, but only wisdom is liberty... —*Will Durant*

Wisdom is the soul's natural food... —*Jacob Anatoli*

Wisdom is like fire: a little enlightens, too much of it can burn... —*Moses Ibn Ezra*

Mere silence is not wisdom, for wisdom consists in knowing when and how to speak and when and where to keep silent... —*Jean P. Camus*

Words

Words are employed to conceal ideas... —*French saying*

Be careful what you say when you say when you talk with words...for words are made of syllables and syllables are made of air... —*Carl Sandburg*

Words can be a power for good—or they can be a power for evil... —*James G. Keller*

We have too money high sounding words, and too few actions that correspond with them... —*Abigail Adams*

A thousand words will not leave so deep an impression as one deed... —*Henrik Ibsen*

Words, like glasses, obscure everything which they do not make clear... —*Joseph Joubert*

Words are, of course, the most powerful drug used by mankind... —*Rudyard Kipling*

Do not say a little in many words, but a great deal in a few... —*Pythagoras*

Words cannot describe everything. The heart's message cannot be communicated in words... —*Ekai*

All words are pegs to hang ideas on... —*Henry W. Beecher*

There is no choice of words for him who clearly sees the truth... —*Ralph W. Emerson*

The tongue of man is a twisty thing, there are plenty of words there of every kind... —*Homer*

Everyone hears only what he understands... —*Johann W. Goethe*

Much wisdom often goes with the fewest words... —*Sophocles*

Words are merely the vehicle on which thoughts ride... —*James R. Adams*

Judge your words before you utter them... —*The Talmud*

Every word carries a vibration that sent out, comes back. A cutting word destroys what a sweet word heals. One spoken word can make or mar the destiny of a being. When heart is put into a word, the word encompasses the totality of love and brings love back. When a word is without heart, it is

cold and empty and will bring back cold and emptiness...
—*Cheryl Canfield*

Words should be scattered like seed: no matter how small the seed may be, if it has found favorable ground, it unfolds its strength... —*Seneca*

Work

If you are called to be a streetsweeper, you should sweep streets even as Michelangelo painted, or Beethoven composed music, or Shakespeare wrote poetry... —*Martin L. King, Jr.*

When our inner self connects to our work and our work to our inner self, the work knows no limit, for the inner self knows no limit... —*Matthew Fox*

It is important to know that words don't move mountains. Work, exacting work moves mountains... —*Danilo Dolci*

It does not matter what your work is on the earth. What does matter is that you do your work with all your heart and with all your strength and all your mind... —*White Eagle*

The desire of one man to live on the fruits of another's labor is the original sin of the world... —*James O'Brien*

The longest–lived men give the longest hours to work...
—*Fred Van Amburgh*

We work to become, not to acquire... —*Elbert Hubbard*

When we use our hands effectively, our hearts are most at peace... —*Akira Yoshizawa*

Have thy tools ready; God will find thee work...
—*Charles Kingsley*

If I had five hours to chop down a tree, I'd spend the first four hours sharpening the axe... —*Abraham Lincoln*

The sum of wisdom is that the time is never lost that is devoted to work... —*Ralph W. Emerson*

I have found no secret of success but hard work... —*Edward Turner*

Thank God every morning when you get up that you have something to do which must be done, whether you like it or not... —*Charles Kingsley*

No man is born into the world whose work is not born with him... —*James Russell Lowell*

Each of us has something within us that needs to be expressed. It may be the desire to play an instrument, paint landscapes, climb mountains, or grow prize–winning chrysanthemums. Whatever that desire is, it comes from our heart and reflects our own unique gifts and abilities... —*G. Jean Anderson*

God sells us all things at the price of labor... —*Leonardo da Vinci*

Worry

Worry is seldom necessary...Worry sprinkles salt in the wound and sand in your mental machinery... —*Fred Van Amburgh*

Worry is spiritual short sight. Its cure is intelligent faith... —*Paul Brunton*

When we are upset about 90 persent of the upset is related to our past and has nothing to do with what we think is upsetting us... —*John Gray*

Worry is a state of mind based on fear... —*Napoleon Hill*

Happy is the man who has broken the chains which hurt the mind, and has given up worrying once and for all... —*Ovid*

The sovereign cure for worry is prayer... —*William James*

Worry is responsible for more disease than all the germs that exist on the face of the earth... —*Thurman Fleet*

Any negative state, like worry, is like your shadow. If you run away, it pursues, but by standing still you see that it has no movement except that which you give it by running away...
—*Vernon Howard*

The worst thing you can possibly do is worrying and thinking about what you could have done... —*Georg C. Lichtenberg*

The more we worry—the more we have something to worry about... —*Tom Seeley*

We abuse our bodies and fill our minds with mental pictures of fear and worry and then find it difficult to understand why we have suffered from a nervous breakdown...
—*Harold Sherman*

Activity is a great antidote for sitting around and worrying...
—*Margo Howard*

I am an old man and have had many troubles, most of which never happened... —*Mark Twain*

Worry is a word that I don't allow myself to use...
—*Dwight D. Eisenhower*

Worry never robs tomorrow of its sorrow; it only saps today of its strength... —*A.J. Cronin*

Do not worry about tomorrow; it will have enough worries of its own. There is no need to add to the troubles each day brings... —*Jesus*

Don't take tomorrow to bed with you... —*Norman V. Peale*

Live only for the moment, worry not, there is no past or future—only now. Worry brings discomfort and pain. It is the downfall of your being... —*Archie Canfield*